What's In A Name

The stories behind some of the best known companies,

products and names in the world.

Woody Vincent

ISBN:1468024736
ISBN-13:978-1468024739

Trademark Acknowledgment

To avoid clutter, I have used the *Associated Press Style Book* guidelines in the use of trademarks, trade names and the like. A complete listing of all the trademarks used in this publication can be found at the end of the book.

to my three beautiful children,

Kathryn, Robert and Thomas.

Table of Contents

Introduction

The **What's In A Name** series of stories was started in the spring of 2009 as part of the long-running *Business for Breakfast* radio program that had been a mainstay of Colorado radio for a number of years. I was the latest co-host of the program and wanted to make a personal contribution. After all, when you're the "new kid on the block," management is always looking to see what you've got.

From the beginning, I thought it would be fun to present the stories with a surprise ending, trying my best to tease and tantalize the listener for the five or six minutes of the narrative. That is the format for most, but not all of the stories although, in a few cases, it was nearly impossible not to let the cat out of the bag. At every step of each story, I do try to give ample clues as to where we're headed, although I occasionally throw in a couple of red herrings just to keep listeners (or readers) off the trail.

I began researching the origins of the trade names of some of the world's largest companies, thinking it might make good material for a five minute radio feature.

It turns out that not every name is all that inspiring; General Motors and Fiat come to mind. GM is pretty self-explanatory and Fiat stands for the *Fabrico Italiano Automobile Torino* or Italian Car Factory of Turin; descriptive but rather perfunctory names at best. It doesn't get much better with companies like BMW which stands for *Bavarian Motor Works,* and so some of those names have been left out in this first edition of the series, although the histories of those companies are indeed fascinating.

Not all the stories are centered around businesses. The stories of Thanksgiving, Santa Claus, the island of Manhattan and the story of Frankenstein come to mind. The Frankenstein story is probably my favorite simply because it contains a reference to the actor, Boris Karloff, that you won't find anywhere else; a tidbit given to my father, Haywood Vincent, Sr., who, in an interview, asked the actor where the stage name, Boris Karloff, came from. Karloff reportedly smiled and gently told my father, "you simply can't have a monster named William Henry Pratt!"

Most of the factual information has come from company websites, which happen to be very informative, although at times self-serving. I found it amusing that the Coca-Cola website makes no mention of the word cocaine, although there is abundant evidence that the coca leaf, legal at the time, was one of the stimulants used in John Pemberton's original formula.

One of the things that struck me from the very beginning of the series is how a simple seed of an idea can lead to something truly amazing. All of the companies that are featured in this book started out with the most humble of beginnings. Even mega-corporations like Exxon-Mobile, part of the Standard Oil trust created by John D. and William Rockefeller grew out of virtual backroom or garage businesses that blossomed into the mammoth organizations they are today. And from that fact, stems the inevitable conclusion that some of the very small businesses we see as we drive to work every day may, in fact, turn out to be the great enterprises that our children and grandchildren will one day embrace as part of the commercial and industrial landscape. I certainly hope so. Despite its occasional mistakes, the system of free enterprise, and the profit motive that accompanies it, have liberated countless millions from a life of endless hardship and poverty.

A couple of final thoughts: most of the stories contained in this book are taken directly from my original manuscripts and, as such, are longer than the actual radio broadcasts. You'll notice that the stories will often start with a phrase like, "today's story is about..." or other obvious references to a live broadcast. I left most of the introductions intact, to retain the sound and feel of the original broadcasts. In that same vein, I decided to leave the "first person" form of the narrative intact as well. The stories read as they were first written.

In some cases, I have added material to the original scripts to clarify ambiguities or omissions that I hadn't noticed at the time of the first broadcasts. It seems that there is almost no end to the editing process. It also turns out that the hardest thing about writing a short feature is keeping it short.

With that in mind, I hope you'll enjoy these little glimpses of the origins of the companies, trade names and in some cases holidays or historical references that we see and hear every day; names that make up much of the fabric of the world that we so often take for granted.

THE MELTED CANDY BAR

There's no question that military invention has been a catalyst for products that eventually made their way into the consumer space. A perfect example is the fact that transistors, cell phones and personal computers are really the result of the demand for miniaturization that was spawned by the space race between the United States and the Soviet Union in the 1950's and 60's. The fact that getting things into earth orbit required them to be smaller and lighter ignited a technological movement from which we still reap benefits today.

Today's story pre-dates the cold war's space race, to a time when the war zone was very much a hot one; a time when the very survival of Great Britain depended on its ability to track enemy aircraft from hundreds of miles away, and how the technology that was developed under those dire conditions eventually made its way into virtually every kitchen in America.

You don't have to look very hard in the field of electronics to discover the name of Nikola Tesla. When it came to electricity, if Tesla didn't invent it outright, he probably had a hand in inventing it. Every time you plug an appliance into the wall, you can thank Tesla. That's because all the power we take for granted runs on something called Alternating Current or AC which Tesla invented.

Tesla was, of course, the Serbian-born genius who also thought up just about everything you could figure out that had to do with radio

1

waves. He probably invented radio, but Marconi received the patent. In the 1920's Tesla had an idea that you could focus radio waves in a concentrated beam and use them in some form of weapon. The so-called "Death Ray." The Greek mathematician Archimedes had a similar idea centuries earlier using a system of focused mirrors and lenses that would use the Sun to set enemy ships on fire. When he first thought of it, Tesla's Death Ray seemed like pure science fiction, but as with any weapons system nobody wants to find out the hard way that somebody else got the thing to work.

In 1933, to the horror of many western leaders, the psychopath, Adolf Hitler, and the Nazi party took control of the German government in a free and fair election. It would be the last election held in Germany until after the end of World War II. The rise to power of Hitler was particularly disturbing to the French and the British who had defeated the Germans in the first World War. They had plenty to worry about as we all know, but one of the things they took seriously was that Hitler might be working on a new super-weapon; not the atomic bomb...the Death Ray.

The Brits were so worried about it that they decided to see if they could build one of their own. The idea was to generate a burst of power that could knock out a city. Fortunately for the rest of us, nobody has come up with a death ray although we're probably still working on it. The Death Ray didn't work because nobody could generate enough power to do any damage. However, the British did come up with something just about as useful. They discovered that they could send out a small, focused beam of radio waves. It wasn't enough to do any damage. In fact, the signal was so weak that when it hit something, it just bounced off.

Now a lot of people have been credited with what came next, but in 1935 an English scientist named Robert Watson-Watt realized that if you could bounce radio waves off of things, you might just get an echo on the way back. And, if you had a very accurate clock, you could measure how long it took to hear the echo and then calculate the distance between yourself and whatever the radio beam had hit. It wouldn't knock down a building, but it would tell you if the Luftwaffe was sending a thousand planes to bomb London. The British called the system, RDF, an acronym for "range and distance finder." The Americans, who had been working in secret on the same thing called it RADAR.

Okay, so big deal! What's radar got to do with my kitchen?

The thing that makes RADAR work is a gizmo called, a magnetron. It's way too complicated to explain, but it sends out little pulses or bursts of electromagnetic energy. It was invented in the 1920's by a guy named Albert Hull, who worked for General Electric. And, believe it or not, you probably have one in your kitchen, unless you're still making popcorn on the stove top.

Anyway, in 1946 another scientist, Dr. Percy L. Spencer was working for the American company, Raytheon. After a long day at the laboratory, shooting juice through a few magnetrons, Spencer made an important discovery. A candy bar that had been in his shirt pocket, had melted, and Dr. Spencer had an epiphany. He deduced that it was the radio waves from the magnetron that had melted the chocolate in his shirt. (I sure hope he had a box of Tide detergent at home, because chocolate is a bugger to get out of a white shirt.)

Radio waves come in all sizes; big ones, short ones and little tiny ones. The little tiny ones are called "micro-waves" and they're what makes radar work. What Spencer had accidentally discovered was that those little microwaves will also jiggle the molecules of anything in their path. They're particularly good at jiggling the water or fat molecules in, say, chocolate. In fact, the microwaves jiggle the molecules so fast that they heat up the fat until it liquifies, which is why the candy bar melted. In a flash, Spencer realized if microwaves could melt chocolate, they could cook food.

3

Spencer took his idea to the managers at Raytheon. I don't know if it was the idea or the ruined shirt that caught their attention, but within a couple of years Raytheon gave birth to the world's first microwave oven. It was a beast that weighed seven hundred pounds and could only hold about a quart-sized container, but it turned out to be something big, indeed. I don't think modern society could live without the thing.

The project was originally called, "the speedy weenie" since cooking hot dogs in sixty seconds was about the only thing the prototype was good for. Later, the company's Amana division came up with something that sounded a little more "high tech"; something we know as...

the *Radar Range*.

MORE PANCAKES, PLEASE

Take a trip through the supermarket and even the most casual observer will recognize the faces and names of all sorts of characters whose images are synonymous with the products they represent, and one of the most famous of those images, one that has been around for nearly 120 years is the subject of today's story.

If the names, Billy Kersands, Christian Rutt, Charles Underwood and Nancy Green mean nothing to you, sit back and enjoy this tale of genuine Americana. Because, while the names behind today's story are some of the most obscure, the product that they ended up creating is a mainstay of the American supermarket and an icon in the field of marketing.

Let's start with Billy Kersands.

Billy Kersands was an African American who was considered the funniest black man in the country from roughly the 1880's to around the turn of the century. A dancer and a comedian, Kersands toured mainly in the Southern states as well as abroad, putting on blackface minstrel shows to the delight of mostly white audiences. His talents were so great in the genre that it was once said of him that a minstrel show without Billy Kersands was like a circus without elephants. Of course, nowadays, the very idea of a minstrel show is offensive to most people and certainly to African-Americans, but at the time, with its buffoonery, slapstick and song and dance, it was an extremely popular form of entertainment. While the Kersands' minstrel show is but a part of history, it would be the name of one of the characters from the show that would eventually end up on the shelves of nearly every grocery store in the country.

About the time that Kersands was making audiences howl, two entrepreneurs in the Midwest came up with a business idea. Initially, there was nothing new about the idea. In fact, it was as mundane as mundane can be. Their names were Christian Rutt and his partner, Charles Underwood. In 1888, Rutt, who at the time was the editor of the St. Louis Post Dispatch, and his friend Underwood bought a flour mill and formed what they called the Pearl Milling Company.

It was supposed to be the first step on the road to riches, or so they thought. Unfortunately, they bought their flour mill just ahead of a bumper crop in the wheat business. There was more wheat than anybody knew what to do with. And too much wheat means too much flour. Rutt and Underwood were practically drowning in the stuff and they had to figure out how to get rid of it.

Fortunately, Chris Rutt had a bright idea. Why not bag the flour and sell it as a prepared food; or to be more specific, a ready-made pancake mix, which is exactly what they did. They sold their pancake mix under a trade name, that they borrowed from a song that was featured in one of Billy Kersands's traveling minstrel shows, that Rutt had apparently seen a few years earlier.

Unfortunately, as clever as the idea was, Rutt and Underwood couldn't make a go of the business and in a couple of years, they threw in the towel and sold out to the R.T. Davis Milling Company in St. Joseph, Missouri. R.T. Davis had a better idea; a marketing gem that the trade publication *Advertising Age* would eventually call a "cultural touchstone" of significant political and social change.

What Davis Milling did was to create a character; a warm and friendly persona played by a woman whose appearance was much like that of the "Mammy" character played so memorably by Hattie McDaniel in the film, *Gone With The Wind*. Hattie McDaniel, by the way, was the first African-American to win an Oscar. But it wasn't Hattie McDaniel that Davis Milling hired. It was a former slave by the name of Nancy Green.

The people at Davis Milling Company dressed Nancy Green in a red bandanna and a white cotton blouse, and introduced her to the world in 1893 at the World Columbian Exposition in Chicago. Nancy Green played the role of a lifetime, literally, one that she would continue to play until her death in 1923. The name of the character was taken from a song in the minstrel show, a song called, " Old Aunt Jemima."

The character was so popular that in 1914 the Davis Milling Company changed its name to the *Aunt Jemima Mills Company*.

Then, sadly, in 1923 Nancy Green was killed in an automobile accident and the character was retired.

But, three years later, the Quaker Oats Company bought Aunt Jemima Mills and in 1937 they decided to revive the character of Aunt Jemima, again in Chicago, at the World's Fair. The new *Jemima* was played by an actress named Anna Robinson, described as a large, gregarious woman with the face of an angel. Several other women would follow in Nancy Green's footsteps and continue the image of the original brand; an image that, in the best of marketing traditions, now extends to frozen pancakes, waffles and a delicious, buttery syrup.

And today to quote directly from their website,

"Aunt Jemima products continue to stand for warmth, nourishment and trust – qualities you'll find in loving moms from diverse backgrounds who care for and want the very best for their families."

I should quickly add that the "Mammy" image has been replaced with a modern African- American woman who looks like she could actually be somebody's aunt. And that's the story of a cultural icon, that was named after a song from a minstrel show, that was borrowed by a newspaper editor and his partner in an effort to get rid of a surplus of buckwheat flour. A cultural icon that has been a mainstay of the American kitchen since the year 1893.

Someone we all know as...

Aunt Jemima.

PUT A POINT ON IT

The other night as I was sleeping comfortably with the windows open on a lovely August night, I was awakened by what I thought was the sound of the city of Denver being bombed by a foreign air force. Fortunately, the city was not under attack. Nor was there any thunder in the area. Neither was there an active volcano or a military weapons train exploding in the vicinity. It was simply the sound of what I assume was the loudest car stereo system on planet earth making its way down my street. It didn't help matters that the sound system belonged to one of my children who, along with his friends will be deaf by the time they reach the age of thirty.

The whole thing made me think about car stereo systems. But first, a little background.

One evening in June of 1752, Benjamin Franklin stood outside his home in Philadelphia during a thunderstorm with the hope of catching a bit of lightening with a kite. It was an experiment that, made Franklin famous but please do not attempt it at home.

Franklin hadn't actually discovered electricity. That honor is generally credited to an English scientist named William Gilbert, who coined the word in 1600, from the Greek word for amber. It turns out that if you rub chunks of amber together, you'll get a spark of electricity and that's where the word comes from. Franklin, by the way, would go on to theorize that electricity generally moves in one direction, although as luck would have it he got the direction backwards.

Now the truth is that, except for electrocuting people, raw electricity isn't really all that much good for anything; it doesn't have many practical applications aside from shocking people and heating things. Where electricity takes center stage in the history of the world is with the discovery of electromagnetism, which was discovered by a danish scientist named Hans Christian Orsted in 1821. Four years later an Englishman named William Sturgeon really got the ball rolling with the invention of the electromagnet. Soon after, a guy named Michael Faraday used the electromagnet to create the first electric motor, and since then the world has never been the same.

That's because, aside from the light bulb and the waffle iron, it's the electromagnet that really harnesses electricity. Electric motors and clocks and fans, power windows, your garage door opener, your blender, the hair dryer, the telephone, the telegraph and the loudspeakers in your car are all based on the electromagnet. (And you though it was just used for dropping old cars into the crusher at the junk yard.)

Anyway, the modern world is centered around the electromagnet. Lose the electromagnet and in pretty short order we're all back to doing things the hard way.

Now, one of the great things to come out of all of this electromagnetism is the reproduction of music, but it took a couple of in-between steps to get there. Thomas Edison is generally credited with inventing the phonograph in 1877. The idea came to him as he was listening to the clicking of a telegraph one day. Edison, if you don't know the story, was a telegraph operator before he invented half the things that we take for granted. The telegraph sounded sort of musical to Edison and within a couple of years he had invented the phonograph. Edison's phonograph was nothing like its offspring of today; including the big boom boxes and car speakers that can wake the dead on a Sunday morning. Edison's machine simply had a large bell speaker attached to it that amplified sound acoustically like an old-fashioned megaphone.

The result was a tinny, thin recording that sounded like the orchestra or the singer was about a half a mile away. Apparently, it was pretty cool if you were living in the 1880's, but by today's standards it was pretty much headed for the scrap heap of history.

Ironically, the actual loudspeaker was invented the same year as the phonograph, by a German named Ernst Siemens who was pretty much the European version of Thomas Edison and whose company still bears his name today. Siemens hooked up an electromagnet to a diaphragm, and voila....the loudspeaker was born; politicians could now make speeches all day without going hoarse. (Not every story has a happy ending.)

Unfortunately for Edison and Siemens, the loudspeaker wouldn't be married to the phonograph for another forty years. That's because until 1906 there was no way to amplify the sound that came from the phonograph.

 Then, along comes an American named, Lee DeForrest. He's a real whiz kid. He invents the vacuum tube amplifier that basically makes it possible to play recorded music just about as loud as you want.

Now, you'd think that the amplifier would get hooked up to the phonograph in a hurry, but you'd be wrong. It would take another twenty years for anybody to make the connection. That's how business works sometimes. It's probably a miracle that chocolate and peanut butter ever came together to make the Reese' s Peanut Butter Cup, but I digress.

Anyway, by the 1920's, thanks to some smart thinking at a company called Bell Laboratories, the musical speaker was finally married to the phonograph and lots of companies got into the speaker business.

One of those companies would eventually make its name putting hi-fidelity sound systems into automobiles. It was a German company called, IDEAL Works, that initially specialized in headphone speakers. It is a company that has gone through a couple of ownership changes over many years and is generally considered top of the line in the competitive business of car stereo systems. You can find it in mostly higher end automobiles, such as Audi, Mercedes and Porsche, although it actually put its first car radio into a Studebaker in 1932.

It was also the first company to offer FM radio for cars in 1952.

A company that started as the Ideal Works in 1923, and then changed its name fifteen years later to reflect its high production standards. And the new name was based on the quality control system the company had used for years. Since only the very best of its original headphones were allowed for public sale, a system was devised to make sure that only the best headphones ever left the Ideal factory. A simple blue dot or blue point was placed on every product that passed the company's high standards, and the two German words for blue dot became the name by which the company is known today...a company known by audiophiles the world over as...

Blaupunkt.

TWO FOR THE MONEY

Today's story presents itself as something of a riddle. The question is what do one of the largest banks in the world, the world's largest brokerage, and the San Francisco earthquake of 1906, have in common?

Let's start with the easy part, and a young man named Amadeo P. Giannini. For the most part, Giannini was simply known by his first initials, A.P. He was born in San Jose, California, the son of Italian immigrants, and he got his start in business as a produce dealer in the Santa Clara Valley. He soon discovered that the big banks in California didn't like to lend money to small farmers in California. It seems that until the housing crisis of 2008, banks really did only lend money to people who didn't need it. At any rate, nature abhors a vacuum and, in 1904, A.P. Giannini opened what he called the *Bank of Italy* in what used to be a saloon in San Francisco. He actually did fairly well; according to company historical records, deposits totaled nearly $9,000 on the first day.

The bank continued to grow until April 18, 1906, when mother nature decided to throw a wrench in the works for most of northern California. That was when all the tension that had been building up along the San Andreas fault broke loose and shook the ground in what we all know as the San Francisco earthquake. Now, what a lot of people don't know about the San Francisco earthquake is that, while the earthquake itself did a tremendous amount of damage, it was the ensuing fire that was most destructive, nearly burning San Francisco to the ground.

This actually proved to be something of a godsend for Giannini and the Bank of Italy. As the city started to burn, Gianinni packed up his small bank's vault and moved it outside the fire zone to his home. (Sounds more like a safe than a vault.) Most of the big banks in San Francisco weren't so lucky.

The fire spread throughout the city, and while the money <u>inside</u> other banks' vaults was actually safe, the vaults themselves were too hot to open for several weeks. But Giannini's vault wasn't red hot at all; it was pretty much room temperature, and he could lend money, which is what he did, and in fact, he lent money extensively; literally setting a board across a couple of barrels on the sidewalk and lending cash to people on a strictly handshake basis. Legend has it that he was repaid every penny he ever lent out during that trying time. In 1922, Giannini renamed his bank to the *Bank of America and Italy*. After a few years, Giannini merged that bank with a bank in Los Angeles which was already called *Bank of America*.

Bank of America remained a mostly California bank for several decades, but in 1983 the company decided to become one of the biggest banks in the country and went on a purchasing binge. It bought all sorts of banks and became the fourth-largest bank in the U.S. and currently has over six thousand branches.

Not satisfied in its quest for growth, in 2008, Bank of America decided it wanted to buy one of the largest brokerage companies in the world; a company called, *Merrill Lynch*. They succeeded in the Merrill Lynch acquisition, and now the company is called *Bank of America/Merrill Lynch*. Okay so much for B of A, where the heck did Merrill Lynch come from?

The Merrill story is a pretty good one of its own but we'll have to settle for the short version. The company was originally started by a guy named *Charles Merrill*, in January of 1914. It had a very clever name, Charles Merrill & Co.. Charlie Merrill had a very good friend by the name of Edmund Lynch. And in 1915, the two became partners and they called their company Merrill, Lynch & Co. But that's just the beginning.

It turns out that Merrill and Lynch were really good at investing; they brought all sorts of things, like a company called *Pathe Films* which later became RKO pictures, and would eventually produce a little film called, *Gone With The Wind*. In 1925, they turned their sights on something less glamorous and cobbled together a slew of mom and pop grocery into the supermarket giant that we know as, *Safeway*.

With each success, the firm continued to expand. In 1940, Merrill, Lynch merged with a company called, *EA Pierce and Cassatt & Co.*, and for a while they were known as Merrill, Lynch, EA Pierce and Cassatt. Definitely a mouthful. A year later, Merrill swallowed up a company called Fenner and Beane, and now the new operation was known as Merrill, Lynch, Pierce, Fenner and Beane. Apparently, Cassatt got bounced off the letterhead.

In 1957, Merrill Lynch dropped Beane's name in order to honor the man who had been running the company since 1940. His name was, Winthrop Smith. And for years, Merrill Lynch was formally known as *Merrill, Lynch, Pierce, Fenner and Smith*.

Of course, the marketing people eventually had to have their say in the matter and they decided that all those names were just too much for anybody to remember. It's also too many letters to try and cram onto a television screen. So, being the clever souls that marketing people are, they abbreviated the whole mouthful back to the original, *Merrill Lynch*. (Advertising people sure know how to get to the point.) And in 2008, Merrill was brought under the Bank of America umbrella.

And now you know how A.P. Giannini's *Bank of Italy* got a big boost from the San Francisco Earthquake, that sowed the seeds for the much larger *Bank of America*, that swallowed up Merrill, Lynch, Pierce, Fenner and Smith, that dropped Pierce and Fenner and Smith, and became....*Bank of America, Merrill Lynch...(whew!)*

The Buffett Way

As is so often the case with these narratives, the origins of many companies often have a very distant connection with the actual business being done today, and this story definitely falls into that category. Because, this story begins with the most fundamental of things, namely the production of cloth, and ends with a company that is one of the most successful investment firms of all time.

If you study much of the industrial history of New England and early Americana, you will soon discover that the textile industry is as deeply embedded in the culture as rock lobster and maple syrup. Textiles were literally the fabric of the New England economy.

The role of textiles is inseparable from the rise of American Industrialism for a number of reasons but the origin of the industry has to do with England.

In the eighteenth century, Great Britain had decided to become the textile supplier to the entire world. An English clergyman named, Edmund Cartwright, had invented a machine called the power loom in the mid 1700's. It was a steam- powered marvel that could belch out endless yards of fabric twenty-four hours a day. It was England's industrial secret weapon, so valued that it was actually illegal to export the machine or even make drawings that would allow it to be built on foreign soil. England had a manufacturing monopoly on cheap milled goods and planned to exploit it to her advantage.

As a result, Colonial Americans were forced to buy textiles and clothing from mother England. This didn't sit well with the colonists, especially in the Northern states of New England who were literally forced to buy the clothes on their backs from the British. Apparently, our forefathers had more problems with the English than just the price of tea. The southern states weren't as bad off, because they had cotton, which they could sell to the English textile mills. So, for the South, it was something of a wash.

The Yankees were stuck with a bad deal. So what did they do? They defied the British and built their own mills. Most of the credit is given to a man named Samuel Slater, a Scottish transplant who was able to reconstruct a working power loom in Rhode Island, largely from memory. A refinement of Slater's loom was developed by a man named Francis Cabot Lowell, for whom the town of Lowell, Massachusetts is named. Milling and spinning were starting to become very big business in America, and after the Revolutionary war, we had more than our share of the world market.

One of the late entrants to the textile business was a man named Oliver Chace who acquired and organized a number of mills around the town of Valley Falls, Rhode Island. He might not have known it at the time, but his company would grow to become one of the largest suppliers of cotton fabric in the world. Chace was the consummate capitalist; he didn't invent the textile business, he grew it and made it more efficient by organizing many mills under the management of his Valley Falls Company.

After Chace's death in 1850, the company stayed in the family and continued to make strategic acquisitions, one of which was a company that had been started in 1889 called, the *Berkshire Cotton Manufacturing Company*. In 1929 the two companies merged and became *Berkshire Fine Spinning Associates*.

As one of the largest textile manufacturers in America, Berkshire enjoyed excellent profitability and continued to make strategic acquisitions. In 1955 it would add yet another milling operation, this time a company that had been founded in 1888 by a man who had made his fortune hunting whales in the Pacific; a man by the name of, Horatio Hathaway.

And it was this combined company that caught the attention of a young protegé of the legendary investor, Benjamin Graham. Graham was the father of what is known collectively as value-investing; the idea that buying under-priced companies is half the battle in making money on Wall Street. Graham's understudy was a down-to-earth no-nonsense young man by the name of Warren Buffett.

What mostly caught Buffett's attention was the fact that the textile company carried a sizable amount of cash on its books; cash that could probably be put to better use. In 1962, Buffett and his investment company, *Buffett Partnership Limited* began buying shares, and by May of 1965 Buffet had acquired a controlling interest. In short order, Buffet quickly overhauled the company changing it from a fabric maker to...of all things an insurance company. That's because the capital requirements of insurance companies allow them to hold on to a lot of money so they can eventually pay claims to their insureds. That money can be invested into all sorts of things and it turns out, it's a pretty good way to make a fortune. The rest is pretty much history.

Buffett's company now either owns or has its hands in just about everything from insurance to clothing, to carpet and paint and soft drinks, even Ginsu knives.

If you're wondering what happened to the Chace family, when Warren Buffett acquired a majority interest, he offered the Chaces a check for fourteen million dollars. Instead, family patriarch Malcolm Chace, Jr. took a chance on Buffett and turned fourteen into many hundreds of millions of dollars. Sometimes change can be good.

And that's the story of how the British government pushed the American colonists into making their own cloth, that started our Industrial Revolution, that eventually created one of the most successful financial holding companies in the world. A company called....

Berkshire Hathaway.

THE REAL THING

By almost any measure, the nineteenth century was a wondrous age of discovery that changed the world, both technologically and socially. Advances in transportation and communication were marvels of the day as the world literally went from horse and buggy to the steam locomotive and the automobile, with the telegraph and the telephone transmitting the news most of the way.

In medicine, too, great discoveries seemed to abound. The acceptance of sterile or a-septic operating practices promoted by Pasteur and Lister saved thousands of lives. Advances in general anesthesia, notably the use of ether, relieved countless surgical patients of needless agony. And during that same era, many pain killing compounds had come into use, the most notable of which were Morphine and later, the drug Cocaine.

Cocaine comes from the coca plant, something that had been mostly a curiosity since the discovery of the new world. Peruvian natives had chewed coca leaves and boasted of its energizing effects, but it seemed to lose most of its potency when it made the long sea voyage from South America to Europe; thus, any "benefits" were generally discounted.

That changed in 1855 when a German chemist named Friedrich Gaedcke figured out how to isolate the active ingredient, an alkaloid chemical that he named Cocaine. Cocaine caught on like wildfire. It was touted as a wonder drug. Sigmund Freud, the father of Psychiatry proclaimed that it was good for just about everything. It would pep you up, make the weak feel strong, make a coward brave. It would even whiten your teeth. What no one realized at the time was that cocaine is highly addictive.

This was unfortunate, because one disturbing development of the nineteenth century was the rise of so-called patent medicines, which for the most part, were neither patented nor medicine. The entire business of pharmaceuticals was virtually unregulated. The general rule of thumb was that if you could put it in a bottle, unless it was an outright poison, you could put a label on it, make almost any claim about it that you wanted and you could sell it, legally. Most patent-medicines were loaded with either alcohol, opium, cocaine or some combination of the three.

Some of the products were simply mind-boggling. They proclaimed to cure everything: cancer, tuberculosis, scarlet fever, epilepsy, venereal disease. If you could catch it, somebody would claim to have a cure for it. The term *snake oil salesman* actually comes from a guy named Clark Stanley, sometimes referred to as the Rattlesnake King. He made his money selling a product called *Rattlesnake Oil,* which he would publicly extract from live rattlesnakes just to show he was on the up and up. For the record, he wasn't. It turned out that his rattlesnake oil was about 99% mineral oil with a bit of red pepper thrown in for good measure. Evidently, it was thought that the "bite" from red pepper would mimic the presumed bite from rattlesnake venom. There's nothing like a good marketing campaign to move product out the door...or off the wagon as the case might be.

One quack by the name of William Radam had a product called the *Microbe Killer* that boldly claimed to, "cure all diseases". It's a wonder anybody bothered to go to medical school. The patent medicine field was as wide open as the American prairie. Anybody with a gift for gab and a mixing bowl could get into the business.

It turns out that one of the people who had a mixing bowl was a chemist in Atlanta, Georgia by the name of John Pemberton. Pemberton had created a few patent medicines on his own, but he had something of an obsession: to create the ultimate medicinal product; a tonic that would be nutritious, beneficial and delicious, all rolled up into a refreshing beverage.

Now, at the time, there was already a beverage called, *Vin Mariani*. It was a cocaine-based wine that was invented by a man named Angelo Mariani, and endorsed by all sorts of celebrities including Queen Victoria, Thomas Edison and writer Emile Zola. They were hooked on the stuff.

But Vin Mariani didn't stop Pemberton. In 1885, he created a rival product that he called *Pemberton's French Wine Coca* that he sold to drug stores in the Atlanta area with some success, but he was concerned that its success might be short-lived. That's because the growing temperance movement in the United States was gaining supporters who believed that <u>anything</u> alcoholic was bad. And any ban on alcohol would mean the end of Pemberton's French Wine Coca.

So, in 1886, Pemberton went back to the drawing board, or in his case, the mixing bowl. He took some extract of coca leaves, which were too bitter for most tastes, and added some sugar syrup, which made the whole thing too sweet. To cut the sticky sweet taste of the mixture, he added a bit of citrus. And to round out the whole thing he added another stimulant, allegedly good for digestion; the fruit of the African <u>Kola</u> tree.

Pemberton stirred the whole concoction together and took it down the block to a place called Jacob's Pharmacy which had a soda fountain on the premises. They added a bit of carbonated water to the whole shebang, and passed around samples to customers in the store, who, although they didn't know it, enjoyed the world's first taste of something that would later be known as, *The Real Thing*.

Jacob's Pharmacy agreed to add the new flavor to its list of offerings. However, the product still needed a name. And that would come from John Pemberton's bookkeeper, a guy by the name of Frank Robinson, who suggested the drink be named after its two noteworthy ingredients. And the name he suggested as you have probably already guessed was: *Coca-Cola.*

Now for the record, Pemberton never made much from his invention. In 1887, he sold the formula to a fellow Georgian named, Asa Griggs Chandler, for the whopping sum of Twenty-three Hundred Dollars. And while we're at it, all but a trace amount of the coca was removed from Coke in 1903, and even that little bit was removed altogether in 1929. One little bit of curiosity; if you visit the Coca Cola website you'll find that, despite a wonderful time-line of the company history, aside from the brand name, there is no mention of coca anywhere.

And today, the little company that literally started in John Pemberton's mixing bowl, is the undisputed leader of the beverage industry, selling over three thousand products with brand names such as *Dasani, Nestea, Sprite, Fresca,* and *Minute Maid* and holds the honor of being the most recognized advertising logo in the world...a product known in 200 countries as...

Coca-Cola.

Popping The Cork

(broadcast December 29, 2011)

With New Years Eve just around the corner, it seems appropriate to talk a little about the celebrations that will take place around the world and at least one of the traditions that seems to be accepted most everywhere.

Celebrating the New Year is actually a little more complicated than you think. Well, the celebrating isn't that complicated; it's the calculation of what is actually the NEW year that gets a little tricky.

In most of the western world, New Years day is celebrated on January 1st and we take that pretty much for granted, but it's not true for large segments of the world's population. The Chinese New year starts around the end of January. The Jewish New Year or Rosh Hashanah comes in late summer or early fall. Much of India and southeast Asia celebrate the New Year shortly after the spring Equinox, which if you think about it makes a lot of sense; after all, spring represents the renewal of the birth cycle for all of nature. It's when a young man's fancy lightly turns to thoughts of love... and all that. Only trouble is that spring is backwards in the southern hemisphere. It Starts in September, when we're starting our fall. Of course, people who live south of the equator don't think they're backwards. They don't even think they're upside down.

But westerners generally celebrate New Years Day as January 1st. We owe that fact, pretty much, to Julius Caesar and something called the Julian Calendar. Nowadays we use something called the Gregorian Calendar, because Caesar's Calendar was off by about two seconds a day. Julius Caesar may have divided Gaul into three parts, but he miscalculated the length of the year by about ten minutes. Doesn't sound like much, but after fifteen hundred years it begins to add up. It was throwing Easter off by a couple of weeks, which made a mess of things in Christian circles. All that was changed in 1584 with a new calendar that was approved by Pope Gregory, which is why it's called the Gregorian calendar.

So, January 1st it is, along with all the party favors, the Big Ball dropping down in Times Square, Dick Clark, the whole Y2K problem that turned out to be no problem at all, new forms from the Internal Revenue Service and of course, last but not least...Champagne! And that's the real subject of today's story. That ever fizzy, ever bubbly libation, the most famous of which sounds like a member of the Corleone crime family when it's mispronounced.

First things first; all Champagne, technically speaking, comes from the Champagne region or "appellation" of France which is located about a hundred miles north and east of Paris. By law and international treaty, only sparkling wines from that region can legally use the word, *Champagne*. Everything else is a sparkling wine.

Champagne itself is something of an accident, both of man and geography. The Romans were the first people to plant grapes for wine-making in the area back in the 6th Century. They filled the whole area with vineyards. The Romans liked to drink a lot of wine.

It turns out that wine-making takes a lot more than just planting grapes wherever you like, and Northern France is not the most suitable area. In fact, the area just south of Champagne, what we call Burgundy, turns out a much more popular red table wine, mostly because Burgundy has a longer growing season and a longer season makes wine taste better.

Up north, the cooler and shorter season makes for a more acidic wine, even though for the most part the same grapes are used. Not great for table wine, but fabulous for Champagne.

While we're at it...A quick lesson in wine-making. Regular wine is made by mixing grapes, yeast and some sugar and letting them sit or ferment in a large vat until some of the sugar is converted into alcohol and a little carbon-dioxide gas. In about a month, the CO_2 sneaks out into the atmosphere and, *voila*, you have a batch of wine. Now, all you need is a bottle and a cork. But, with champagne, the fermentation takes place *inside* the bottle, and all that CO_2 turns into...champagne bubbles. Champagne was actually first created accidentally in the early 1500's when some Benedictine Monks bottled their wine too soon, before all the fermentation had finished. Pretty soon they noticed that their wine bottles started exploding from the pressure of all that gas inside. In fact, Champagne was originally called, the *Devil's Wine* because, well, the bottles kept exploding. But the wine was fantastic...as one monk put it...it felt like drinking stars.

Then, around the late 1600's another Benedictine Monk developed a number of improvements in the whole Champagne process including a stronger bottle and the invention of that little metal collar or *muselet* that holds the cork in. We'll get to his name in a minute, but he is generally considered the father of Champagne as we know it. And that turned out to be a godsend for the northern vineyards and champagne, because the French Royal family developed quite a taste for the stuff. So much so that King Louis XIV had a glass of Champagne every morning until quite late in his life.

Within a few years, the Champagne business caught on like hot cakes, and wineries such as Taittinger, Moet et Chandon and Veuve Cliquot Ponsardin all sprang up in the 1700's and are still in existence today.

Then, in 1921, an Englishman name Laurence Venn proposed an idea to the company of, Moet et Chandon. He suggested they make a special small batch or *cuvee* of their very best champagne with the strict understanding that it would not be released for public sale for fifteen years. The idea was so well received that millionaires all over the world snapped up a few hundred bottles, some of which have never been opened. Soon, other champagne makers followed suit and now, all the best houses have their own premium brands; the best of the best.

But it was the Moet version that started it all, and in the best of traditions, they named their premium *cuvee* after the man who had been credited, although somewhat inaccurately, with the creation of Champagne; a Benedictine Monk born in 1638, whose name was Dom Pierre Perignon. And if you're very lucky this New Year's eve, and have about $150 dollars on you, perhaps you and a close friend can sample a bottle of...

Dom Perignon.

ADVENTURES IN GOOD EATING

I thought it would be fun for today's "What's in A Name" to pose something of a trivia question; something along the lines of the game show, "Who Wants to be a Millionaire."

Okay, so let's get started. We'll pretend that you've already made it past all the preliminary questions and now you're playing for the big million dollar prize. I'll even throw in one of the show's lifelines to help you along, although after all is said and done, it won't really help much. Ready? Here we go. Here's the question:

Of the following four commercial brands that are found in every American supermarket, only one is the name of a real person.

The names are: Charlie the Tuna, Uncle Ben, Duncan Hines and Betty Crocker. Alright, now you can use your lifeline. Since you're pretty much on my dime, I'll have to pick the lifeline for you and I think I'll go with the fifty/fifty lifeline...you know, where we eliminate two of the four possible answers.

Let's start with Charlie the Tuna. Not a real person, but it makes a kind of fun story. Charlie the Tuna, in case you're too young to remember, was the cartoon mascot of the Starkist Tuna Company who appeared in nearly ninety television commercials. He was always dressed up as a sophisticated hipster, at least as sophisticated as a tuna fish can be. He would try to convince the announcer that he had good taste, only to be told that Starkist, *"didn't want tuna with good taste; they wanted tuna that tasted good."* Charlie the Tuna was the brainchild of a copy writer named Tom Rogers of the famed ad agency, Leo Burnett. But Charlie the Tuna was pure fiction. Not a real person...sorry Charlie...as the ads always closed. By the way, according to the Washington Post, in a bit of pure irony, Tom Rogers, Charlie's creator died a few years ago while...swimming...in the family swimming pool. He was 87.

One down, three to go. Next comes Uncle Ben, the neatly-dressed, bow-tied symbol of Uncle Ben's Converted Rice, which is a company owned by the Mars family. The same Mars family that makes M&M's, Three Musketeers and Snickers candy bars, to name just a few.

Uncle Ben is a little bit trickier. After all, surely there are a lot of people named Ben who are somebody's uncle. The current Chairman of the Federal Reserve Bank, Benjamin Bernanke is often called "Uncle Ben", but I'm pretty sure he doesn't have anything to do with the rice business, unless you count the currently high prices of commodities. The Mars Company says that there really was an "Uncle" Ben sometime after the civil war who was known for the high quality of rice that he grew on his acreage, and that he is the inspiration for the brand, but the story seems to be suspect. After all, most people in the western world have last names, and the nickname "Uncle" was often used as a patronizing term for any elderly African-American in earlier times. So, I am discounting the veracity of "Uncle Ben" as an identifiable individual.

So, now we've eliminated our first two choices, which leaves us with Betty Crocker and Duncan Hines. I will give you a hint; one of them is based on a real person with a little bit of a name change, and the other was a very real person indeed.

First, the almost real person. If you've never heard of the Washburn Crosby Company, don't worry. I hadn't either, but up until 1928 it was one of the largest grain milling companies in the U.S. It started out as the Minnesota Milling Company in 1856 before the Civil War, but was soon acquired by a guy named Cadwallader C. Washburn who changed its name. Ownership has its privileges. In 1877, Wasburn took on a partner named, John Crosby, and the Washburn Crosby Company was formed. By the way, if you're from the Twin Cities and you've ever listened to WCCO radio, it got its call letters from Washburn Crosby Co. or WCCO, after the milling company bought the radio station. Cool Huh?

Anyway, Washburn Crosby was a very innovative company, and in 1921 they wanted to create a figurehead, a persona, who could answer the many letters that the company received from customers about recipes, nutrition and other aspects of the company's flour products. The task of naming that fictional character was given to a home economist by the name of Marjorie Child Husted who combined two names which, together, are an icon of American marketing. She wanted the first name to be as American as apple pie, and selected the last name from a much-loved director of Washburn Crosby, William Crocker, and the final result that can be seen on grocery shelves every day was: Betty Crocker.

By the way, in case you're interested, Washburn Crosby went on to become a behemoth in the food processing industry, when in 1928, it merged twenty-six other companies under its umbrella and gave itself a new name...a company called *General Mills*.

And that leaves us with the only other possibility, which by now you may well have forgotten, so I'll try not to remind you until the very end.

The real person in our collection of four, is the man whose name is still found on cake mixes, brownies, cupcakes, you name it...if you can mix it in a bowl and toss it in the oven, his name is on the box. It's so ubiquitous that you would think the name belonged to a baker.

But you'd be wrong. Because the correct answer to our little trivia quiz is a name that belongs to a man who started his career as a traveling salesman working for a Chicago-based printing company. Umm...yummy! So how did <u>his</u> name get on the cake mix box at the supermarket?

Well, our traveling salesman was on the road for so many years and had eaten at so many restaurants that he decided to publish a record of his travels with a rating system for restaurants, both good and bad. And in 1935 he published a journal of his gastronomical odyssey, which he called, *Adventures in Good Eating*. It was so successful that he published a follow-up that also rated hotels and motels across the country.

With a reputation for good taste, in 1952 he teamed up with the Durkee Bakery Company of Homer, New York, and a year later he sold the rights to license his name on other baked goods as well.

The name went from one owner to another, most notably to Proctor and Gamble, but now is the property of a company called Pinnacle Foods Group which has the exclusive rights to use the name; which as you have no doubt guessed is the answer to today's trivia question. Sorry Charlie, there's no million-dollar prize; just the satisfaction that if you answered correctly, you answered...

Duncan Hines.

Starting Off With A Bang

In the year 1620, the English philosopher and academic, Sir Francis Bacon gave credit to three things that had changed the course of history and the evolution of civilization. They were: paper, the compass and a unique combination of chemicals that have come to be known as gunpowder. Those three along with the invention of printing were all the achievements of the ancient Chinese, although Bacon himself was unclear as to their origins. Three hundred years earlier another Englishman named Roger Bacon, no relation, had discovered a workable formula for the gunpowder that the Chinese had invented, probably in the 9th century A.D., during the Tang dynasty.

The Chinese had been looking for what they called the Elixir of Life. What they discovered would soon become just the opposite; a medium of death and destruction that would change the world forever.

While the Chinese had been content to use gunpowder in fireworks, to ward off demons and ghouls from the afterlife, it didn't take long to make its way to the battlefield; probably first used by the Mongols as they swept over the great plains of central Asia. Then, sometime in the 13th century a man called William of Rubruck, a Franciscan missionary and Flemish Ambassador to the Mongols, is thought to have given their formula for gunpowder to his good friend, Roger Bacon.

And before you know it, before you could say hand-grenade, the leaders of Europe, who were always looking for new and clever ways to kill one another, had the formula along with the will and the wherewithal to make cannons, guns, bombs, grenades and just about anything else you can think of that can go boom and kill people.

While it was President Eisenhower who is officially credited with warning Americans of the growing military industrial complex, the fact is that the ties between business and the military really pre-date Ike by a couple of centuries. The military had the money, and business made the gunpowder and the guns. You don't have to connect too many dots to get the big picture.

Gunpowder was big business by the late 1700's, which was an unusually nasty time in European history, and French history in particular. The French Revolution, unlike our own, was nothing short of mob violence on a national scale. It is probably best known for the Reign of Terror in which somewhere between sixteen and forty thousand so called "enemies of the revolution" were put to death under the guillotine. So many people were executed under what the radicals called, "the national razor." that nobody could keep count. That's a lot of enemies of the revolution.

One of the men who narrowly escaped the chopping block was a chemist who had personally defended King Louis and the royal family from the blood thirsty mob. This ultimately led to his becoming a man marked for death. He had been an understudy of the great chemist, Antoine Lavoisier. If that name means nothing to you, it probably should. Lavoisier was a French nobleman and scientist who discovered and named both oxygen and hydrogen. He was a chemist who was so dedicated to the study of science that after being convicted of crimes against the revolution, asked for a short stay of execution so that he could finish several ongoing experiments. Unfortunately for him, he was told by the judge that the revolution had no need of scientists at the time, and that was the end of Dr. Lavoisier. For the record, a year and a half later, the government conceded that it had acted in haste. Not much consolation when your head is in a basket.

But his student, the son of a watchmaker, survived the revolution and in 1802 at the age of twenty-nine, fled his native France for the safe haven of the newly formed republic of the United States. There, on the shore of the Brandywine River in the State of Delaware, he opened his first factory, making use of the knowledge of gunpowder manufacturing that he had learned from Lavoisier.

The company prospered beyond measure and, in fact, supplied most of the gunpowder to the United States during the War of 1812 and to the Union side during the Civil War. The company was so successful as an explosives maker that in the 1930's it was hauled before Congress to face accusations of war profiteering and labeled a merchant of death. Nobody seemed to mind when they were helping us fend off the British at the Battle of New Orleans.

Over the years it has also lent its considerable wealth and expertise to peacetime applications that have benefited Americans and people the world over. It has long since expanded its business from the manufacture of gunpowder and high explosives, and is now a mega-conglomerate whose products are household names and sold worldwide under such trademarks as, *Nylon, Teflon, Kevlar, Mylar, Lycra* and *Corian* to name just a few.

It is a company that is directly responsible for nearly ten percent of the employment of the entire State of Delaware and whose offspring remain one of the most influential families in America.

A company that trades on Wall street under the ticker symbol DD, a tribute to the initials of its founder, Eleuthere Irenee **D**upont **d**e Nemours, although most of us know it simply as...*DuPont.*

It's a Doosey

Today's *What's in a Name* is the story of two brothers born in the 1870's who emigrated to the United States from their home town in Northern Germany in the late 19th century. By all accounts, although they lacked formal education, the brothers Fred and August were accomplished mechanics and self-taught engineers who excelled in what was the cutting edge of technology at the turn of the century, namely the design and construction of automobiles.

They set up their first car factory...if you could call it that in Des Moines, Iowa and began work on their first projects. They never really formed what you could call an assembly line, all of their production cars were hand-built from the ground up and in the early stages of their company the focus was entirely on racing cars.

The cars had a reputation for quality and durability. In 1914, their efforts started to pay off when racing legend and later aviation legend Eddie Rickenbacker drove one of their hand made cars to a tenth place finish in the Indianapolis 500. Over the next several years, their cars would win many prestigious auto racing titles including the French Grand Prix in 1921 and would take the checkered flag at Indy in 1924, 1925 and 1927.

Their cars were masterpieces of engineering, employing innovative features that are still in use today such as four-valve cylinder heads and four-wheel hydraulic brake systems designed by brother Fred. By the way, all cars today use some version of Fred's braking system, but since they never applied for a patent, they denied themselves of the fortune they could have made from this single invention.

As early as 1920, hand made cars bearing their name were being purchased by celebrities mostly in the entertainment field. One of the early owners was silent film star, Rudolf Valentino. Unfortunately, as the failure to get a patent on the much acclaimed and much copied braking system would suggest, the brothers were a lot better at making cars than they were at running a business.

While their reputation had become widespread, they lacked the capital needed to run a successful car company, and in 1919 they actually sold the rights for the use of their own name to a couple of entrepreneurs named Van Zandt and Rankin who apparently didn't know how to run a company either, which probably explains why you've never heard of anybody owning an 1919 Van Zandt.

Anyway…the car company that was to become a legend barely survived through 1925 and faced extinction several times. Then something happened that was to change the face of the automobile industry forever.

In 1926, along comes an American businessman named E.L. Cord, the same guy that gave us the Cord and the Auburn Speedster. Cord bought the company and the name and told brother Fred that he wanted to make the best automobiles in the world. The goal was to produce 500 cars per year that were to compete with Rolls Royce, Mercedes and a number of cars that have long since fallen into oblivion. By the way, according to automobile historian Griffith Borgeson, Cord "didn't want brother Auggie around", so Auggie got the boot and the newly formed car company began with only Fred involved.

And, thus, was born one of the most revered automobiles of all time…bearing the name of the two brothers who had brought it into the world: the Deusenberg Model J; a car so expensive that during the 1920's you could spend nearly twenty thousand dollars to get your hands on one. To give you an idea of what twenty grand was like in that day, a doctor's salary averaged about three thousand dollars a year. Today, doctors can spend that much in two weeks just on malpractice insurance, and that's before they pay for any of those outdated *People* magazines lying around the waiting room.

According to *Wikipedia*, only 481 of the *Model J* Deusenbergs were ever built. Lucky owners included: Greta Garbo, Clarke Gable, Gary Cooper, Tyrone Power, King Victor Emanuel of Italy, William Randolf Hearst and his gal pal Marion Davies. Al Capone owned one, (apparently there's money in bootlegging), and so did The Duke of Windsor, who as you may know, gave up the throne as King of England to marry the commoner, Wallis Simpson, but kept the Duesenberg.

There are fewer than four hundred of the cars in existence today. Jay Leno owns one of them. If you'd like to have a look at it you can go to a website called, *JayLenosgarage.com*…cool huh?

Today, a Deusenberg will fetch close to two million dollars at auction. Not bad for a couple of brothers, who came to America with nothing but a dream and perhaps a desire to make a name for themselves.

And that's the story of how two brothers and a businessman named E.L. Cord combined their talents into creating the automotive legend known as....

Deusenberg.

Utopian Turtletop

What do *Anticipator, Thunder Crester, Pastelogram, Intelligent Whale, The Resilient Bullet, and Utopian Turtletop* all have in common? They were the suggestions for the name of a new automobile submitted by the Pulitzer Prize winning American poet, Marianne Moore. Moore was a modernist poet who had been commissioned by The Ford Motor Company to come up with the perfect name for its new wonder car; the car that Ford's advertising agency, the renowned Foote, Cohn and Belding, described as, "the most beautiful thing that ever happened to horsepower."

For the record, it was a dog. The ads should have read, the biggest dog since Lassie. And, in the end, it would cost the Ford Motor Company the tidy sum of two hundred and fifty million dollars. In 1958, that was some real money.

The idea behind the new dream car was spawned in the early 1950's. Ford, anxious to wrest market share away from the dominant General Motors, wanted to create a new line of cars that would fill the gaps between the namesake Ford and the Lincoln-Mercury marques. And that was actually part of the problem. Ford tried to do both. Instead of picking a spot between either Ford and its upscale Mercury division <u>or</u> between Mercury and the luxury Lincoln brand, the management at Ford decided they could have their cake and eat it too; create a new car line from scratch and have it fill all the gaps in the Ford lineup.

In marketing terms, it was a branding error. Meaning, either you're a luxury car or you're an upscale economy car, but you can't be both.

Unfortunately, nobody bothered to tell Ford that, and what they ended up with was the mother of all marketing blunders, which as you may have guessed was called the *Edsel.*

But that's just the beginning.

The origin of the name is very simple simple; Edsel Bryant Ford was the only child of Henry and Clara Ford. A bright and inventive youngster, Edsel Ford was personally responsible for many of the innovations that helped secure the Ford Motor Company's place in automotive history.

He had been responsible for the purchase of the Lincoln Motor Car Company in 1922 and had added the Mercury line as part of a marketing strategy to keep Ford from being outflanked by GM, which boasted some six lines of cars at the time including Chevrolet, Oldsmobile, Pontiac, Buick and the now defunct LaSalle.

It was during Edsel Ford's tenure as head of Ford that the first mass-produced V-8 engine was introduced; the legendary Flathead V-8 that so improved the performance of Ford cars that the bank robber, John Dillinger, once proclaimed that if he was ever caught, he would be driving a Ford.

Edsel Ford would go on to introduce numerous innovations at Ford until his untimely death of stomach cancer in 1943, just five months shy of his fiftieth birthday.

Which brings us back to the car that bears his name still, as a collector's item.

The marketing people at Ford had no idea what to call their new dream car, and from the looks of it, the design team didn't have much of an idea on what it should look like. If you look at it today, it seems like a mishmash of design ideas cobbled together with spare fenders and parts from the Ford plant and then run through the chrome house a couple of times for good luck.

The distinguishing hallmark of the Edsel was its unique vertical grille, which the public called the *horse collar*. Compared to, say, the E-type Jaguar of 1963 which is consistently rated as the most beautiful automotive design of all time, the 1958 Edsel was a stylistically cumbersome hulk of a car that had the grace and elegance of a block of lead. Well, maybe a block of lead with a horse collar.

It didn't help that the car was a mechanical nightmare; often assembled in so much of a hurry that new vehicles would arrive at dealer showrooms needing brakes and steering wheels.

The Edsel made its debut in September of 1957, a month ahead of the normal time for new car introductions, surrounded by so much hype and mystery that it was almost certain to be a disappointment. And disappoint it did. When *E-Day,* as it was called, finally arrived, the letdown was almost palpable. Throngs of would be buyers showed up at Edsel showrooms only to flee the premises with their checkbooks still in hand. A massive advertising campaign and even a television program starring Bing Crosby and Rosemary Clooney couldn't spare this behemoth from a one-way trip to the junk yard.

Still, why the name Edsel? The answer is quite simple. Nobody at Ford could agree on a name. They solicited names from everywhere. The folks at Foote, Cohn and Belding came up with a list of 18,000 names which they whittled down to a mere six thousand ; names like Citation, Corsair, Ranger and Pacer all had a shot, but none made it to the final product. They were so desperate that they hired the aforementioned poet, Marianne Moore, whose most forgettable gem was the *Utopian Turtletop.* She might have been the only person on the project who knew less about cars than the marketing people at Ford.

And then something happened that changed the course of automotive history. It's a lesson that should be taught in every business school in America; the lesson that whenever the boss puts in his two cents worth, nobody is going to raise an objection. And so the story goes, that a man named Ernest Breech, who just happened to be the

Chairman of the Board of the Ford Motor Company, having dealt with the impossible list of names and the endless indecision threw up his hands in frustration one day and said, "why don't we just call it, Edsel." And in that single instant, the agonizingly painful process of naming a car that Washington Post writer Peter Carlson called, "the flop heard round the world" came to an end.

Ford had hoped to sell 200,000 Edsels in the 1958 model year, the actual number was just over 63,000. By the time Ford finally pulled the plug in 1960, just over 118,000 cars had been sold altogether, the last three thousand nearly given away by dealers anxious to rid themselves of the things.

The ads read, "once you see it, you'll never forget it" and sadly, that was the truest thing ever said about...

The Edsel.

Black Gold

Today's story starts back in the late 1840s in a town called Titusville, Pennsylvania. What's special about Titusville is oil. Now, they didn't really have any oil wells back then; what they had was oil that just seeped up out of the ground. And, in fact, they called it rock oil. Unfortunately, you had to wait for the oil to bubble up out of the ground of its own accord, and then you basically scooped it up and poured into a barrel. It was kind of hit and miss, not a really great business model.

Back then, oil was really just used for two things; lubrication and illumination in lanterns. For the most part people still used whale oil in lanterns, but let's face it, it's a lot easier to scoop oil off the ground than it is to go chasing down a whale.

Then, in 1857, along comes a guy named Edwin Drake, he calls himself "Colonel" Edwin Drake although he's not really a colonel of anything. He just wanted to impress all the people in Titusville, which apparently he did. Drake has a great idea that is better than scooping oil off the ground. He thinks, "hey, why don't we drill a well?" Seems obvious now but nobody had the idea until 1857. So Drake and a couple of buddies start drilling a hole in the ground much the way he'd seen people drill for salt. Unfortunately, the hole kept filling up with dirt.

Undismayed, Drake had another great idea and he invented something called the drive pipe. It's that steel cylinder that the drill goes into. You put a new 10 foot section of drive pipe into the ground and it keeps the dirt from filling in the hole. Pretty clever idea. Sadly, Drake never patented his invention and so he never got rich from it.

Anyway, after a couple of years of hard work, The Colonel hits a gusher, and that's pretty much the start of the oil business. The little town of Titusville is pumping out as much as 3,000 barrels of oil a day.

Now, crude oil isn't much good to anybody until it's refined into something more useable such as kerosene, for example. It turned out that kerosene was a lot cheaper than whale oil, so cheap that people started using it in their lamps and lanterns. And one of the people making all that kerosene is a guy in Cleveland, named, John D. Rockefeller, along with his brother William.

By 1870, the Rockefeller boys were doing pretty well. In fact, they were refining about ten percent of all the kerosene being made in America! Nonetheless, John D. wanted more. So, he teamed up with a couple of other businessmen and they formed a company called, Standard Oil Company of Ohio, with an eye to owning the entire refining business.

The first thing Rockefeller did was buy out nearly all the oil refineries in Cleveland. Then he made a deal with the railroads. He promised to deliver sixty oil tank cars worth of kerosene every day if they would give him a bargain-basement rate. The railroads thought that was a great idea. They'd get a heck of a lot of business, and get rich. The only problem was that Rockefeller's competitors couldn't compete with Standard Oil's rate with the railroads, and so they started going broke, which is a pretty good way to make a lot of enemies.

By 1880, the Rockefellers and their business partners were refining about ninety percent of all the kerosene in America, and the original Standard Oil had divided itself into a passel of mini-Standard Oil's; there was Standard Oil of Ohio, Standard Oil of New Jersey, Standard

Oil of New York, Standard Oil of California, here a Standard there a Standard...everywhere a Standard Oil.

Anyway, Rockefeller did a lot of nasty things which were legal back then, but are illegal now mostly thanks to something called the Sherman Antitrust Act.

After a while, a lot of people got tired of the way that the Rockefellers did business. They decided that Standard Oil had gotten to be too big. The newspapers really hated the Rockefellers, and they pushed hard to break up what was called the Standard Oil Trust. I'm giving you the short version, otherwise we'll be here all day.

Anyway, in 1909 the US government sued Standard Oil under the Sherman Antitrust Act accusing the company of being a monopoly. The government won the case and Standard Oil had to break itself up into, catch this, thirty-four different companies. Now, we are getting to the heart of the matter. Two of those companies were Standard Oil of New Jersey and Standard Oil of New York.

Standard Oil of New York would eventually change its name to Mobil Oil, and that didn't seem to bother anybody.

Standard Oil of New Jersey changed its name to *ESSO*. You might remember the old ESSO billboards from the 1950s. Well, if you think about it, ESSO sounds a lot like the letters **S** and **O**, which sound like the initials for **S**tandard **O**il. In fact, ESSO reminded everybody of Standard Oil so much, that a lot of individual <u>states</u> wouldn't let them use the name, ESSO at all. That's how unpopular the Rockefellers were.

So, in some places the companies were called *ENCO* or *HUMBLE* or *CARTER* or a bunch of other names. Anyway, it was all pretty confusing, and the company wanted to have one name for the whole kit and caboodle. They were going to go nationwide with ENCO, until somebody realized that in Japanese, "enco" means "stalled car." Not a great idea for a company that sells gasoline.

So, they came up with a brand-new name, and that name was, *EXXON*. They even hired a really famous designer named, Raymond Loewy, to come up with the logo. If you don't know who Raymond Loewy is, he's the same guy who designed the Coca-Cola bottle.

Well, to make a long story short, in 1999 the Justice Department does a complete legal flip-flop and decides it's okay for oil companies to get big again. So guess what happened? Exxon and Mobil Oil merged. And they became Exxon-Mobil, which is what they are today. And, in 2005, according to Forbes Magazine, Exxon-Mobil became the biggest company in the world. As of 2011 it's actually number two...behind...of all things...*Apple Computers.*

And that's how Standard Oil of New Jersey and Standard Oil of New York went from being part of one great big company, split into two smaller companies, and then changed back into one great big company...again; a company called...

Exxon-Mobil.

Absolutely, Positively

Today's story involves one of those company trade names that have become synonymous with the product or service they represent. There's actually a word for it: *genericized*. Words like Coke, which has become synonymous with any cola drink. In the South, a coke can mean any kind of soft drink at all, except for maybe Dr. Pepper, which you have to ask for by name; and preferably three times a day, at 10, 2 and 4. I have friends from the south who will ask, if you want a coke, and then say, "I have real coke, seven-up or ginger ale."

Xerox was probably the best example of a genericized trademark until so many people got into the copier business. Nowadays, people just make copies of documents, but twenty years ago they made Xeroxes. Kleenex is still used as a noun, and I seriously doubt if that will change, well at least not among men. I, for one, am not going to ask anybody to hand me a box of facial tissues when I can just ask for a Kleenex. Not me, not ever. Nor, am I going to mention that Kleenex is a registered trade mark of the Kimberly Clark Corporation every time that I want to blow my nose. I may well buy the store-brand of Kleenex, but only because I'm cheap. If my nose is sore, I'll spring for the real thing just because generic tissues feel like sandpaper.

Okay, with that out of the way, let me state for the record, this is not a story about Kleenex. This is a story that starts with a bus company, which funds a restaurant chain then takes a detour through New Haven, Connecticut and then ends up on just about every airport runway in the world. Oh, and just for grins, they also happen to be in the copying business.

In 1925, a truck salesman in Memphis, Tennessee by the name of James Frederick Smith received a heavy duty truck as a gift from his former employer. Smith, an entrepreneur by nature, had a great idea to take the body off of the truck chassis and convert the vehicle into a passenger bus, and thus fill a need for public transportation in that area of the rural south. Smith had seen the success that public carriers like Greyhound had enjoyed and thought he would go into competition. By 1931, Smith's company had turned into a major success, operating some sixty coaches throughout the Tennessee and Mississippi area. So successful, in fact, that in 1931, Smith sold the majority of what he now called the *Smith Motor Coach Company* to Greyhound who renamed it, *Dixie Greyhound Lines*. The Smith family continued to own a minority interest until 1948 when they sold their remaining share to Greyhound due to a death in the family.

Smith wasn't content being a minority owner of a burgeoning bus line company. So he decided to branch out. If you've ever been to a *Waffle House* restaurant, you might be interested in knowing that the concept originated in a southern restaurant called, *The Toddle House,* which was headquartered in Memphis and the creation of none other than James Frederick Smith. One of his former employees actually started the Waffle House a few years later.

Toddle House turned out to be a very successful business idea. Each restaurant was small, and generally featured ten or twelve stools curved around a single lunch counter. If you think about it, it was a business that flowed naturally from the bus company concept. After all, people in buses need to eat. Why not fill the need with a no-frills, quick service lunch counter? One unique feature was that all customers paid on the honor system. They dropped the money they owed into a box as they left the Toddle House. You have to wonder how well that system would work today. My guess is that they'd have to change the name to The Chapter 11 House.

Well, as it turned out, James Frederick Smith didn't have to worry about it because he died a few years after opening the restaurant chain but not before his wife gave birth to a son, Frederick Wallace Smith, in 1944; the subject of our story.

As a child, the younger Fred Smith had shown an interest in airplanes. Not all that unusual in the 1940's as, in many ways, it was the Golden Age of aviation. Howard Hughes had circled the world, Amelia Earhart had died trying, and the end of World War II was ushering-in the Jet Age. The world was becoming smaller and smaller, and it would be only a few years before the airplane would replace the railroad train as the preferred method of long distance passenger travel. Of course, freight traffic would always be dominated by railroads. Of course.

Fred Smith attended private school and High School in Memphis and, in 1962, entered college in New Haven, Connecticut at Yale University, where fellow classmates included future Presidential rivals George W. Bush and John Kerry. Fred Smith was reportedly considered for the post of Defense Secretary in the Bush Administration.

Anyway, in 1966 Smith would receive his bachelor's degree in economics, but while he was an undergraduate student at Yale, he wrote an economics paper that would change his life and the way the entire world does business.

That's because Fred Smith wrote a paper detailing an ambitious plan to create an overnight delivery service, using airplanes to deliver time-sensitive documents with a promised delivery time of 10:00 AM. As the ads would later proclaim, "when it absolutely, positively has to get there, overnight."

Legend has it that Smith received a "C" for his paper although that story may be part of the fabric of modern corporate folklore. He would later recall, somewhat in jest, that he "probably received a "C" since that, according to Smith, is what what he usually got.

After Yale, Smith joined the Marines where he served as a ground officer and learned the basics of military logistics; the science of getting things where they need to go...on-time.

And then, in 1970, using part of the 4 million dollars of his inheritance, (apparently, it pays to own part of the Greyhound System), Smith bought an airplane maintenance company called, *Ark Aviation* and turned the focus of the company into used airplane sales. A year later using the rest of his inheritance and about 90 million dollars in venture capital, he founded the company that he is famous for, and started limited overnight air service to twenty-five cities in the U.S. Apparently somebody thought that term paper was worth more than a "C". And in case you haven't guessed, that little start-up company was called...

Federal Express

which now calls itself *FEDEX*, which like COKE and KLEENEX and XEROX, has become part of the English Language. Oh, and the copier part...in 2004, FEDEX bought the copying and printing company KINKO's...which it now calls, FEDEX Office.

Flying Saucers

On June 24, 1947, a private aviator named Kenneth Arnold reported what he described as, "nine disk shaped metallic objects flying in a chain-like pattern" over the skies near Mt. Rainier in the state of Washington. It is generally accepted as the first sighting of an unidentified flying object or UFO, and ever since that time, people have been on the lookout for aliens in some kind of saucer-shaped contraption. Sci-fi movies like *The Day the Earth Stood Still, War of the Worlds, Earth vs. The Flying Saucers* and even the more recent *Close Encounters of the Third Kind* all have some form of flying saucer. When Hollywood and the UFO crowd see something in the heavens, you can pretty much bet your bottom dollar, it's going to be a flying saucer. Never mind that here on the primitive old Earth, nobody has ever been able to create a working flying saucer. The best thing mankind has been able to come up with for space travel, has been a rocket ship to get <u>off</u> the Earth, and the Space Shuttle to get back. But heck, what do we know.

In fact, aside from something called the *Avrocar*, which turned out to be a kind of forerunner to the hovercraft that floats across the English Channel, only one disk-shaped flying device has ever successfully navigated its way over the surface of the earth, and it has usually done so at an elevation of about six to ten feet above the ground, and has always been flung by a single human; which brings us a rather obscure inventor by the name of, Walter Frederick Morrison. While you may have never heard of the late Mr. Morrison, it is almost certain that you have personally used his most famous invention. It, or some imitation of the original, has been tossed around on playing fields on all seven continents.

Morrison was a Los Angeles building inspector by profession, but he had an inquisitive and inventive nature. He came by it naturally; his father had invented a staple of the automobile industry, the sealed beam headlight that is standard issue on all cars. The younger Morrison served in World War II and was, in fact, a prisoner of war in the now infamous Stalag 13 on which the TV sitcom *Hogan's Heroes* was based.

After returning from Germany, Morrison took a job as a carpenter, but his inventive mind kept tugging at him to, well, invent something. And in 1948, with the world fascinated by the idea of flying saucers, Morrison set out to create a hand-held model. He started with a pie tin and welded a steel rim inside to give the disk a bit of flying stability. Results were mixed, so Morrison turned to fabricating a flying disk out of plastic resin, which allowed him to form a curved edge on his flying disk. And thus was born something called the *Pluto Platter*.

That 'platter' was very popular by the mid nineteen fifties. So popular that it caught the attention of a couple of entrepreneurs named, Richard Knerr and Arthur "Spud" Melin. Knerr and Melin had created a new toy company that they called *Wham-O*. Wham-O had experienced its original success with the legendary *Hula Hoop,* and they wanted to find a followup product. They approached Morrison and ended up buying the rights to the Pluto Platter which, after a couple of years was christened with a new name inspired by, of all things, the baking pans of a pie company in Bridgeport, Connecticut.

It turns out that students at nearby Yale University had amused themselves for decades by flinging pie tins across campus, but not just any pie tins. They favored the unique invention of a baker who, in the 1870's, had the clever idea of embossing his company's name on the underside of his pie tins. It was a marketing gimmick that was supposed to serve as a reminder that it's a lot easier to <u>buy</u> a freshly baked pie than it is to <u>bake</u> one. There's no telling how well the marketing ploy worked, but one thing is certain; it left a lot of pie tins with the company's name on them lying around on the Yale campus. (Nowadays, the company would probably receive a complaint from the Environmental Protection Agency and be forced to pay a fine.)

After a few years, the name on the bottom of the pie tin became synonymous with a hand flung flying saucer. Then, in 1957, the pie company went out of business and Wham-O picked up the trademark, made a slight spelling change for legal purposes, and applied it to Fred Morrison's old Pluto Platter...a name that will forever honor the founder of that Bridgeport pie company...

a man named William Russell *__Frisbie.__*

(By the way, Wham-O changed the spelling to *Frisbee*.)

The Best A Man Can Get

Our story starts in the town of Fond du Lac, Wisconsin, in 1855, with the birth of baby boy named, King Camp Gillette. The family did not stay in Wisconsin all that long, eventually moving to Chicago where things went pretty well until they were more or less wiped out by the great Chicago fire of 1871.

Chicago emerged better than ever from the fire and so did the Gillette family, but before we get too far along in the story I want to talk about a product called the bottle cap.

Today we take bottle caps for granted; they are mostly twist-off affairs but prior to about 1890 bottle caps involved a complicated mechanical contraption. You basically had a cork and a large, heavy wire mechanism attached to a bottle that held the cork in place for things like beer and soda pop.

In 1892, a rather clever man named William Painter, of Philadelphia, decided that the old bottle cap model wasn't a very good idea, and set out to create something better. He invented the bottle cap design that we are all familiar with today. It's that familiar little round piece of metal on top of the bottle that, when you turn it upside down, looks kind of like a little crown. That's what Painter invented and it looked so much like a little crown that he called his company, guess what, the *Crown Cork and Seal Company*. They're still in business today.

Okay, so the great thing about Painter's bottle caps, as opposed to the old system, is that bottle caps have to be replaced. If you've ever tried to get one back on a bottle, it is pretty much a lost cause. Well, the bottle cap company was going so well that, in the early 1890's, they opened up a plant in Chicago, and guess who they hired? King Gillette. He got a job selling William Painter's "Crown" bottle caps, and that's where he caught on to the idea that the way to make money is to sell something that has to be replaced.

Of course, this is not an entirely revolutionary idea. After all, farmers and coal companies have been selling consumable products since the beginning of time. But back in the 1890's, it was a pretty radical idea. Skilled craftsmen made things that were supposed to last. Nobody had ever heard of "planned obsolescence." At any rate, Gillette saw the writing on the wall, and since he didn't want to sell bottle caps all his life, by the mid 1890's he came up with an idea that he thought would make <u>himself</u> rich.

It was a new twist on an old idea, and, of course, it's the idea for which we know the Gillette Company; namely, the safety razor. Now the safety razor had actually been around for quite some time. It was invented by a Frenchman by the name of Jean-Jacques Perret, who got the idea looking at a carpenter's plane; you have just a little tiny bit of a blade extending from the base of a piece of metal so that it would barely scrape the surface of a man's skin. It's a lot safer than a straight razor which, if you've ever tried to use one, you'll soon discover is a real good way to slash your face to shreds.

The problem with early safety razors was that they used a heavy steel blade that had to be taken down to the hardware store and re-sharpened every couple of weeks. Well, for most men, this was just a big hassle and the safety razor really never caught on that well, which is why, when you look at pictures from the 1800's, most men have beards.

So, along comes King Gillette and he has two really great ideas. The first idea is the creation of the actual razor blade for the safety razor. Gillette has a brilliant idea to make <u>disposable</u> blades made from a continuous roll of a very thin metal. You can use them for about a week and then you throw them away. It took about five years to develop the technology to make the whole process work, but in 1901, Gillette was granted a patent on the system and opened the *American Safety Razor Blade Company*. A couple of years later, Gillette changed the name to the *Gillette Safety Razor Blade Company*. He even went so far as to have his own picture trademarked and when you bought a packet of razor blades you got to see what King Gillette looked like. But that's not the greatest thing that Gillette did.

Gillette also created an entire marketing scheme that is still used today. It's the same marketing scheme that manufacturers of laser printers use to sell their products. Gillette recognized that it was razor <u>blades </u>not razors that were the key to his business just as printer companies realize that it's ink, not printers, that make all of their money. (Just as a footnote, there is so much profit in the ink that goes into laser printers that it is actually more expensive than human blood.)

Anyway, Gillette's second great idea was to <u>give</u> <u>away</u> the safety razors and then sell customers razor <u>blades</u> for the rest of their lives. The business model is actually so successful that marketing books refer to it as the "razor and blades" business model.

Well, to make a long story short, men loved the new safety razor and its disposable blades. It caught on like hotcakes. By 1915, Gillette was selling about seventy million razor blades a year. In 1918, the U.S. Army signed a contract with Gillette, and King Gillette became the supplier-of-record to the military. It's not exactly the beginning of the military industrial complex, but it sure made a heck of a lot of money for Gillette.

When you think about it, King Gillette really transformed the look of the American male population. As I mentioned earlier, prior to the invention of the safety razor, most men had beards. If you take a look at photographs from the Civil War era, everybody had a beard. Men had mutton chops, sideburns, full beards, mustaches you name it, but if you take a look at pictures taken from the 1920's almost no one has a beard. America became a clean-shaven nation, and that, for the most part, is still the case today.

Gillette has renamed and re-invented its product many times, in 1947, it introduced a product called the *Super Speed* razor, and in the mid-1950s, it introduced an adjustable razor.

In the 1970's, they introduced the world's first twin-blade razor, called the *Track Two,* and since then they've come up with all sorts of names like *Atria, Sensor* and *Mach 3,* to name just a few. Gillette also produces things like *Oral-B* toothbrushes and *Braun* electric shavers along with a whole slew of other things.

 In 2005, Gillette was purchased by Procter and Gamble, and the Gillette **Company** ceased to exist, although Gillette still remains the number one <u>brand</u> name for shaving supplies worldwide.

And that's the story of one man who had an idea that he could make money by selling something that eventually had to be thrown away and replaced; the story of a company called...

Gillette.

(whose advertising slogan for years was,

"the best a man can get.")

Search and Ye Shall find

I never cease to be amazed at the marvels of the information age. The idea that, with a few keystrokes on a personal computer, the average American can either discover the complexities of almost any academic subject, or simply find a good restaurant, boggles the mind; and all from the comfort of the family room, the college dorm or while on the road.

How on Earth did we get here? What was it that brought the magic and the power of the internet to our fingertips?

Despite what you may have heard, it didn't come from Al Gore. Now, to be fair, the former Vice-President never claimed to have <u>invented</u> the internet. He said that he "took the initiative in creating it"; promoting legislation that helped move the internet into the mainstream, and for that he deserves a genuine round of applause.

But, if you have to look for a starting point, a good place would be with...the Russians.

That's because in 1957, the Russians, or more properly the Soviet Union, launched something called *Sputnik* into space. If you've never heard of Sputnik, let me just say how much I envy your youth. Sputnik was the first satellite...ever! It was a spherical radio transmitter that was about the size of a basketball and weighed a couple of hundred pounds, and it scared everybody...and for good reason. If the Russians could get a satellite up into space, they could get a bomb up there. And there's no telling how much mischief you can get into when you have a bomb looking down at everybody. The space race was on and America was starting out in second place.

Anyway, the folks in Washington thought it would be a good idea if all the scientists in our country could link up their computers into one great big network, so that we could coordinate our efforts to keep up with those pesky Russians. So, we set up something called the *Advanced Research Projects Agency*, or ARPA for short. And, in pretty short order, they created something called ARPA-NET which was the forerunner of the internet.

Now, in reality, the internet is just a big maze of wires, not unlike the phone company, only, in the beginning it was a <u>private</u> network. It was just for the Department of Defense and the University whiz kids who were doing research for the DOD. It was about as far from <u>user-friendly</u> as you can get. If you weren't a computer geek, the internet was about as useful as ketchup on a bicycle seat.

But all that changed in the early 1990's because of an Oxford graduate named, Tim Berners-Lee. Berners-Lee managed to put all the different technical elements together that we take for granted as the internet, and he called it, the **World Wide Web**. World Wide Web is where that silly "www" comes from that everybody wonders if they still have to mention every time they refer to a website. For the record, you can drop the three double-U's. Young people already know that; the old dogs will keep on saying it, which proves that they really can't learn new tricks.

It's the World Wide Web that makes the internet work for the rest of us. Different addresses for different websites; color, sound, blogs, maps, video clips and all that. The web takes all the work out of the internet. It's kind of like the menu at a restaurant. We don't really need to know what goes on in the kitchen; we just want to know what's for dinner.

Now, in spite of all of its amazing technology, the web would still be pretty hard to navigate without something called...*the search engine*. Something like...Google, or Netscape, for example. It's the search engine that finds what you're looking for on the internet.

It was created in 1990 by a student at McGill University in Montreal named, Alan Emtage. He called it, "Archie" because it was supposed to be short for the word, *archives*. It's a lot better pun when you see it in print. Archie was soon followed by rivals which were called Veronica and Jughead. I kid you not.

Anyway, Archie, Veronica and Jughead were Okay, but they were a far cry from what we use today.

In the early days, finding anything on the internet was still pretty much hit and miss. If you searched for, say Chinese Food, you could end up with either a list of restaurants or a story about food production during the Ming Dynasty. That's because the early search engines combed the entire web looking for the number of words in a file that matched the word that you entered. It was a reasonable approach but still fairly primitive, because when you think about it, while a report on food in China might use those words a dozen times, a Chinese restaurant might only use the phrase "Chinese food" once.

What the world needed, and badly, was a better search engine; and in 1996, two Ph.D. candidates at Stanford named Larry Page and Sergey Brin were about to create it. They had a better idea: instead of looking for the <u>number</u> of identical words on a web page, they looked at <u>who</u> was looking for them. It's what's called a <u>back-link</u>. For example, if <u>I</u> did a search for Chinese food, it might be logical to infer that I was looking for a restaurant, but if the <u>U.S. Department of Agriculture</u> did the same search it might mean something else. It's a lot more complicated than that, but the concept led to MUCH better internet searches. It allows me to get an order of Moo Goo Gai Pan instead of a crop report when I do a web search.

And it was just what the internet needed. Page and Brin thought they had created the best thing since sliced bread, so they shopped it around to places like *Yahoo* and *Excite dot com*. Both companies turned them down. (They apparently already knew everything they needed to know about search engines. Kind of reminds you of Decca Records turning down a band called, *The Beatles*, doesn't it?)

Then, a guy named Andy Bechtolsheim, the co-founder of *Sun Microsystems* had an interview with the boys, listened to their story, and wrote a check for a hundred thousand dollars on the spot. Larry and Sergey were about to change the world. Now all they needed was a name for their little search engine company.

And the name they picked was based on the altered spelling of a mathematical term that describes a one, with a hundred zeroes after it. They changed the spelling of the original word, incorporated in 1997, and in August of 2004, went public with a stock offering that turned themselves into billionaires and many company employees into overnight millionaires.

A little company that started as a research project, and is now listed as a verb in Webster's Dictionary. Something we know as...

GOOGLE.

(The original word is spelled googol)

Settling Bets

(first broadcast on March 17, 2011, St. Patrick's Day)

If you've ever had the dream of getting rich, one good way to do it is to sell a couple of million books; and so today, I'd like to tell the story of one of the best selling books of all time. I should quickly point out that the two books that have been printed more than any other are, of course, The Bible and The Koran. But today, I want to focus on something a little more on the commercial side of publishing. And, keeping with today's Irish theme, I thought I'd like to talk about the most successful and possibly the most famous book ever to come out of the Emerald Isle.

First, just for fun, a little bit of history. The best selling novel of all time is generally thought to be Charles Dickens' classic, *A Tale of Two Cities*. In case you've forgotten, it starts out with one of the most memorable lines in all of English Literature, "It was the best of times...it was the worst of times." It turned out to be the start of some pretty good times for Charles Dickens; since more than two hundred million copies have been sold since its first publication in 1859.

The best selling <u>American</u> book of all time is, *The DaVinci Code,* which was written by Dan Brown and has sold something like 87 million copies. It's a distant second to *A Tale of Two Cities*, but who's counting.

The American novel that had the longest run as a best-seller was General Lew Wallace's epic, *Ben Hur, A Tale of the Christ:* which was published in 1880 and remained the best-selling novel for some fifty-six years until it was replaced by Margaret Mitchell's "immortal tale of the old South", *Gone With The Wind.*

The best selling Irish author is C.S. Lewis who wrote the *Chronicles of Narnia* among others, but he's really from Northern Ireland, which doesn't count now does it?

So, let's get down to brass tacks and talk about something truly Irish on this St. Paddy's day. I already mentioned one way to get rich. Here's another: sell a couple of billion bottles of beer. Now, wouldn't it be great if we could find something that combined beer and books? Well, guess what...you're in luck!

Because today's story is arguably the best selling book of its kind. I say, "arguably" because that's what the book is all about. It was created to settle arguments, and is considered the definitive source for settling disputes on the most wide ranging subjects. It has sold in the neighborhood of one hundred million copies since it was first published in 1955.

Along with the usual statistics on sporting records, it also contains fascinating and obscure facts on every kind of world record; things like the oldest bungee jumper, the world's largest pocket knife, the most miles covered in a single day on a unicycle, and on and on. It has undoubtedly led to a great deal of close to insane behavior as people the world over have sought to gain entry into its ever-expanding list of records, things like the record for holding the most rattlesnakes in a person's mouth at the same time. Apparently, everybody has a dream.

You probably already have a good idea of where we're going, but I promise not to make it official until we get to the end of the story.

In 1759, a gentleman by the name of Arthur Guinness started brewing ale at the St. James Gate Brewery in Dublin. The ale was a rich dark alcoholic beverage that is known today as stout. Over the past two and a half centuries, the company has sold various versions of its popular ales and is the originator of *Guinness Stout, Extra Stout, Special Export Stout* and a whole host of others including *Guinness Draught.* The Guinness name has been synonymous with a stout ale since its inception, and is the best selling ale in all of Ireland...even though in 1932 the company actually moved its corporate headquarters to London. Is there no shame in this world?

So, what does any of this have to do with the book publishing business?

Well, Arthur Guinness didn't live forever, and after a lengthy line of successors, the company came to be run by another gentleman; this one a South African industrialist by the name of, Sir Hugh Eyre Campbell Beaver.

One day in May of 1951, Sir Hugh, who was the managing director of the Guinness Breweries at the time, was part of a hunting party, stalking wild birds in the southeast of Ireland, when an argument broke out as to which was the fastest game bird in all of Europe. Was it the Grouse or the Golden Plover? My, the things that rich people spend their time thinking about.

The question seemed so important and perplexing at the time that Sir Hugh carried it with him all the way back to the Castlebridge House in Ireland where he and his party continued to ponder the important question. There is suspicion that drinking may have been involved in the course of the discussion.

At any rate, before anybody could say, "who cares", a business was born. Because it occurred to Sir Hugh that this surely couldn't be the only argument going on in all the pubs in Ireland. Surely not. Perhaps there should be a book that contained the definitive answer to the Grouse question and any similar arguments that might arise as a result of alcohol intoxication.

Sir Hugh's concept was turned into a reality when a Guinness employee suggested that two twin brothers by the name of Norris and Ross McWhirter should do the initial research to compile answers to various questions that might come up in the course of an evening's drinking. The McWhirter brothers had been running a London-based fact-finding company at the time and were perfectly suited for the job. And thus, in August of 1955, the very first 197 page edition of a book that would become a best-seller by the following Christmas, was published under the now familiar title that we all know as...

The Guinness Book of Records

(which is now known as The Guinness Book of <u>World</u> Records)

Road Hogs

In 1867, just two years after the end of the Civil War, an American inventor by the name of Sylvester Roper had an idea. And with it, he created something that had never been seen before. He attached a steam engine to a bicycle and in doing so invented...the motorcycle.

It was an elaborate contraption complete with a large boiler, a charcoal firebox and a set of cranks attached to the rear wheel. The thing worked well enough that Roper received a patent for it. And while I will quickly confess to being a motorcycle enthusiast, I wouldn't want to have the thing fall on me with all that charcoal and boiling water. But great ideas sometimes have weird beginnings. Unfortunately for Sylvester Roper, great ideas occasionally have sad endings. In June of 1896, Roper was killed while test riding a new improved version of his steam motorcycle. So much for improvements.

But the concept was a good one. So good, that within a few years of Roper's steam cycle, a German named Gottlieb Daimler attached an internal combustion engine to a bicycle, and is generally credited with inventing the modern motorcycle. Daimler, by the way, is the same guy whose company would eventually merge with another German firm and produce the automobile that most people know as, Mercedes-Benz.

Anyway, the blueprint for future motorcycles had been created and, theoretically, anybody with a bicycle and a little mechanical aptitude could make one. And in 1901, two young men from Milwaukee, Wisconsin did just that, creating one of the great partnerships in

American business history. It is the story of two childhood friends who started with a dream that became an icon in the world of motorcycling; the story of William S. Harley and Arthur Davidson.

In 1901, William Harley decided to make a powered bicycle; a regular pedal bike with a motor attached. He and his friend Arthur Davidson labored over the machine for almost two years before completing the project with the help of Davidson's older brother, Walter. The idea was to make a bicycle with a power assist that would get up the hills in the Milwaukee area. Unfortunately, the first machine was underpowered and couldn't get over the hills without using the pedals. Harley and the Davidson brothers chalked up the failure as a learning experience and started working on a new improved model.

In 1904, the boys unveiled a 405 cc motorbike that they assembled with the help of an aspiring young engine maker by the name of Ole Evinrude...the same Evinrude who would become famous for his motorboat engines. The new bike was a success and even competed in a motorcycle race at the Wisconsin State Fair in that same year.

By January of 1905, Harley and Davidson were offering mail order, assemble yourself, motorcycles, and by April of that year they were selling fully-assembled bikes on a limited production basis.

The boys were on a roll, so to speak, and in 1907 they introduced what would be the beginning of their legacy; the V-twin engine which they debuted at the Chicago Automobile Show.

Business continued to soar, so much so that, by 1913, just ten years after the creation of their very first machine, Harley and Davidson sold over 16,000 motorcycles. The product was reliable and popular. The U.S. Army even ordered them to be used along the Mexican border in its effort to capture the Mexican revolutionary, Pancho Villa. Then along came World War I and again, the Army gave Harley Davidson a shot in the arm by ordering 15,000 motorcycles to aid in the war effort.

The Great Depression took its toll on Harley, slashing sales by nearly 80 percent. But, eventually, the Depression came to an end and, after the dust settled, Harley Davidson remained as one of only two American motorcycle manufacturers to survive the decade; the other being long-time rival, The Indian Motorcycle Company.

World War II would bring more military business, and after the war, the motorcycle enjoyed a revival until its image was blemished by one particularly nasty incident in 1947, in the town of Hollister, California.

An event called the *Gypsy Tour Motorcycle Rally* made its way through Hollister, with thousands of bikers descending on the little town, which was clearly unprepared to handle the sometimes unruly crowd. Bikers were everywhere, often sleeping on the sidewalks and getting into brawls. After all was said and done, some sixty people had been injured, three of them seriously. The incident was played up by newspapers all over the country and it served as the basis for the movie, *The Wild One,* which starred Marlon Brando and Lee Marvin. The image of motorcycles in general was definitely tarnished, and as the number-one manufacturer, Harley Davidson caught a great deal of the negative fallout. It would take years to recover. As the years passed, Harley-Davidson became associated with motorcycle gangs and misfits. Even *The Beach Boys*, arguably the most all-American of rock bands, chose a Honda when it came time to pay tribute to the motorcycle.

About that same time, the image of Harley-Davidson took another bruising when it was accused of trying to stifle competition by asking the Federal government to put huge tariffs on imported motorcycles, from Italy, Germany and Japan.

In 1969, things got worse. Harley was purchased by the American Machinery and Foundry Company, or AMF for short. The AMF years are generally considered to be the low point in Harley's history. AMF sought to increase profits by streamlining the manufacturing process and cutting the workforce. Soon, the once venerable Harley Davidson was known by such slurs as *Hardly Ableson*, and *Hardly Drivable*; all coming at a time when Japanese rivals Honda and Yamaha were making great inroads in the American market. Sales declined to the point that HD nearly went bankrupt.

By 1981, enough was enough. A group of fifteen investors bought the company for eighty million dollars. The company set out to restore its reputation with better products and limited production. In all fairness, it did get a little help from Congress, which imposed a stiff tariff on all large imported motorcycles. That group of investors was put together by Willie G. Davidson, the grandson of the company's co-founder. Harley Davidson had come back to its roots.

And today, the iconic brand continues to be a cherished and favored symbol of motorcycle enthusiasts worldwide.

The company that literally started in the backyard of two childhood friends and whose lifelong partnership built an empire and a brand that still bears their names...

a symbol of the great American open road....a company called...

Harley-Davidson.

(by the way, Harley-Davidson trades on the New York Stock Exchange under the symbol *HOG* which stands for, *Harley Owners Group*)

For The Next Twenty Minutes

This is the story of a broadcasting phenomenon that has made its way into the homes of millions of Americans. It is as addictive as any soap opera or game show. The people who love it, truly LOVE it, and the rest of us seem to enjoy it from time to time as well. It is the bargain hunters' dream and it has made its founders rich, and enriched the lives of countless inventors and entrepreneurs whose products were first seen on this cable network's twenty-four hour sales floor.

In the 1970's, a gentleman by the name of Lowell Paxson owned an AM radio station in the city of Clearwater Florida. Now, in case you've forgotten, the 1970's marked a transitional period in the fortunes of radio. AM radio, which had been the king of the airwaves since the time of Marconi, was starting to lose market share to the much better-sounding FM. And as audiences began to migrate over to the FM dial, AM radio station owners began to feel the pinch in lost advertising revenues. Paxson was headed for tough times and he knew it. So he decided to make a programming change.

He changed the format of his station from 'easy listening' and started something of an on-the-air flea market where sponsors could sell their wares directly to the public via radio. The show was called, *The Bargaineers*. I guess it was supposed to sound like 'Buccaneers', but without the eye patch and the parrot.

It wasn't the first time anybody had tried a program like that; most smaller markets had something similar that either featured new goods from retailers or worked like a flea market where locals could unload their trinkets, treasures and trash.

Anyway, *The Bargaineers* was an immediate success. People are always shopping for bargains and the show seemed to fit the bill. Local sponsors would pay a fee to promote their products on the air, announce in-store specials for the day and so on.

Then one day, something unusual happened. A local merchant who had no money to pay his bill, offered instead to pay with...can openers; a boatload of avocado-green can openers. The task of selling them was given to an on-air personality by the name of Bob Circosta, and with Circosta's natural charm, the can openers sold like hotcakes. They sold out.

So far, so good. Now as most retailers know, it's easier to sell an item on television than it is to sell it on radio, since the audience can <u>see</u> what it's buying. So, the next logical step for Lloyd Paxson and The Bargaineers was to migrate over to the small screen. But the trouble with TV advertising at the time was that it cost too much. There were only a relative handful of TV stations compared to the thousands of radio stations across the land, and that limited supply of media outlets meant higher costs.

Then, a sea change took place in the field of Television broadcasting. It was the advent of cable. Cable TV broke the back of the big TV networks' virtual monopoly of the airwaves. And in 1982, with financial help from a local real estate developer named Roy Speer, a new cable channel was born that featured the soon to become super pitchman Bob Circosta and a host of others on a local Florida show that called itself...the Home shopping Club.

Within three years, the "Club" had expanded itself into the now familiar,

Home Shopping Network,

that has sold billions of dollars in merchandise and undoubtedly countless thousands of avocado green can-openers.

Big Blue

In the movie, *2001: A Space Odyssey,* a lifelike and paranoid super computer named Hal does its best to kill two astronauts who are headed for the planet Jupiter, and while writer Arthur C. Clarke has always insisted that the initials H-A-L stood for *Heuristic ALgorithmic,* he also acknowledged that never a week went by that some movie buff did not see the connection between HAL and the subject of today's story. I'll get back to HAL in a few minutes, but first, let's step back in time about a century or so to the year 1890.

One of the requirements of the U.S. Constitution is that every ten years a census be taken so that the membership of the House of Representatives can be adjusted to reflect changes in the makeup of the population. The daunting task of a census is that, unlike a survey which bases its conclusions on mathematical estimates, a census is supposed to be an exact count of everybody in the country.

And in the year 1890 it was a big job. America had been filling with immigrants who were only too eager to seek fame and fortune in the New World. Most people thought that the population had swollen to 75 million, but, in fact, the number was far smaller; just under 63 million. I mention the 1890 Census in particular, because it was in that year that the final count of the population had been conducted electronically for the very first time; tabulated by an ingenious device, the so-called *punch card reader* that had been invented by an American statistician named, Herman Hollerith. Hollerith's tabulation machine and the company that he built around it would serve as the centerpiece of a giant conglomerate formed by a man known as, the Father of Trusts, a man named Charles Ranlett Flint.

Charles Ranlett Flint was an icon of American finance whose deal-making prowess at creating large companies from a mosaic of smaller firms led him to create, among other things, *The U.S. Rubber Company*. After that, he combined a mishmash of chewing gum companies into what became known as *American Chicle*. But his greatest accomplishment was to cobble together a combination of calculating, weighing and tabulating companies that would eventually grow into one of the largest companies in the world: the massive corporate conglomerate that can rightfully claim to have pioneered the information age; a company that started out as the *Computing, Tabulating and Recording Company,* or C-T-R, in the year 1911.

In many ways, CTR is the poster child for the art of strategic acquisitions; an amalgamation of different business that merged over the years to become the behemoth that it is today. Names like the *Tabulating Machine Company, The International Time Recording Company* and the *Computing Scale Company* would eventually be rolled into Charles Flint's CTR.

By the year 1914, CTR had grown to be something of an unmanageable giant, with its many divisions operating independently of one another. So, Flint made a change at the top. And that change would make history. He hired a man named, Thomas Watson, Sr., who had been the number two executive at the powerhouse, National Cash Register Company. Watson's mission was to bring order to the diverse corporate interests that had become CTR, and which by now had included adding machines, tabulators and industrial scales, as well as meat and cheese slicers.

Working from the company's headquarters in Endicott, New York, Watson, whose constant mantra at CTR was the single word, "THINK", would help double company sales in just four years, and by the mid 1920's, if it could be counted, sorted and put down on paper...CTR did it. They counted everything, company records, hourly wages, railroad passenger tickets, school teacher's schedules, you name it and CTR counted it.

By 1924, the company was doing business internationally and changed its name from CTR to something that would reflect its expanding world wide footprint. The name by which it is known today.

In the 1930's, its equipment was used to track the records of tens of millions of wage earners under the newly created Social Security System.

It was one of the first companies to offer group life insurance, survivor benefits and paid vacations to its employees.

Toward the end of World War II, the company made its first foray into the business that is its hallmark today, the business of computers. Its first real computer was a nearly five-ton beast called the Mark I, created in 1944 that could barely add and subtract. Within a few years, advanced models could handle some 17,000 calculations per second, and the world was on its way to large scale main-frame computing. By the mid 1950's, the company's model 7090 was handling a quarter of a million calculations per second, and was bought by the U.S. Air force to keep track of the Soviet Missile threat.

From there, the list seems endless with innovative products that included the legendary *System 360* family of large computers, the seemingly magical *Selectric* typewriter that used a rotating ball instead of mechanical keys, the supermarket scanner that uses infra-red lasers to read the price at the checkout stand, the ATM, the magnetic stripe on your credit card, as well as the floppy disk and the computer hard drive that ultimately paved the way for the personal computer revolution that we take for granted today, and a form of artificial intelligence that the company named, *Watson*.

Which brings us back to the film *2001*, and the computer named HAL; because if you take the *H* and the *A* and the *L* in HAL...and increase each letter by a single increment, you will end up with an *I*, a *B* and an *M*, the initials of a company whose nickname is *Big Blue*, and is officially known as...

International Business Machines.

(Just a little aside, Watson added <u>International</u> as a bit of one-upmanship to his former employer, <u>National</u> Cash Register)

Tennessee Whiskey

I was watching a NASCAR race on Television the other day, and it got me to thinking about whiskey. It got me thinking about whiskey for two reasons. Number one, it was after noon on a weekend and I was thirsty; and number two, I was reminded of the fact that NASCAR owes its origins to the moonshine business although they don't like to make a big deal about it.

Anyway, the fact is that the story of Whiskey and in particular, American Whiskey has a fascinating history and is the subject of today's story.

Most people that I know who drink whiskey, drink Scotch, and the more they know about Scotch, the more they are inclined to drink single malt Scotch. Some Scotch drinkers are real snobs about it. If you mention that you like *Glenlivet*, they'll roll their eyes. Ask for a *Cutty Sark* or a *Johnnie Walker* and they might need medical assistance.

There are seemingly infinite brands of what I consider good Scotch, although as a rule I'm not a Scotch drinker. Sooner or later, if you get to be real good at being a Scotch snob, you'll buy yourself a bottle of *The Macallan*, and then you'll really be the cat's meow. As I was researching this story, I saw a fifth of "The Macallan" online in a LaLique crystal decanter that was fifty-five years old, and selling for $20,399.00. If you're a real good negotiator, you might be able to grind 'em down to Nineteen Nine. The best part about the website was that it had that familiar little icon that reads "add to cart," just like you were buying a twelve dollar novel on *Amazon*. What would we ever do without rich people?

By the way...not that you'd drink from a twenty thousand dollar stash of Scotch in the first place, but I wouldn't recommend it anyway since, over time, the lead in the crystal leaches out into the liquor and gives you lead poising.

But, the fact is, that the Scots invented whiskey, and it's pretty good for keeping you warm when the weather is cold and miserable on the Scottish Highlands, which is pretty much all the time. (When Ben Hogan won the British Open at Carnoustie in 1953, he had to wear three sweaters, and that was in the middle of the summer. No wonder they drink.)[1]

Anyway, this isn't really a story about Scotch. It's a story about Bourbon or what most people think is Bourbon. I started with Scotch because it was the Scots who first brought whiskey to America.

What makes Bourbon unique is the fact that it is made from corn. It's made from corn because in the late 1700's, farmers in the area south of the Ohio River Valley, or what the Cherokee Indians called, "Kentucky," had so much corn on their hands that they didn't know what to do with it. They couldn't eat it all, and it cost too much to ship it somewhere else. So what did they do? They distilled it, and turned it into whiskey.

Bourbon, is actually made from what's called a "sour mash" of grain, malt and water that's added to the corn later. The whole idea of "sour mash" came from a Scottish chemist named James Crow[2] in the 1830's. The "mash" works kind of like the starter in sourdough bread. You take a little from the last batch and use it the make the new batch. Dr. Crow perfected the formula and when you buy a bottle of *"Old Crow"* Bourbon, that's where it got its name. But wait...we're still a long way from the end, because I said that this wasn't really a story about Bourbon.

Bourbon gets its name from Bourbon County, Kentucky. Bourbon county was originally part of a huge tract of land that was part of Virginia. The name, *Bourbon,* is an homage to the Royal Family of France, or the *House of Bourbon*. That's because during the American Revolutionary war, King Louis XVI of France sent money and material to the Americans to help us defeat the British. In gratitude, Virginia renamed one of its counties, "Bourbon," and part of that original land would later became part of the Commonwealth of Kentucky. Louisville, Kentucky is named in honor of King Louis, just in case you were wondering.

The term *Bourbon whiskey* was first used by a guy named Jacob Spears. He bottled his own corn whiskey in Bourbon County, Kentucky and called it 'Bourbon whiskey.' Nowadays, there's a Federal Standard for calling something Bourbon. It has to be *"mostly corn-based and it has to be made from liquor that has been aged in brand new oak barrels that have been charred on the inside."* And you can't use the barrels twice. Don't worry, they don't just throw the barrels away. They sell them to the Scots for aging Scotch Whiskey. Ain't capitalism grand?

Anyway, that's pretty much the story of Bourbon, but not the end of our story. Because our story moves one state east of Kentucky to Tennessee, where the best known American Whiskey is produced.

In the mid 1800's, the folks in Lincoln County, Tennessee added a special twist to making Bourbon. They had the idea to filter the whiskey through a thick layer of maple charcoal before putting it into the oak barrels for storage. It was called the *Lincoln County process*. And the result is a unique kind of Whiskey that is legally known as, *Tennessee Whiskey*.

Currently, only two distilleries produce Tennessee whiskey. One of them is called George W. Dickel and the other carries the name of a man who in 1871 built his original distillery in the Town of Lynchburg, Tennessee.

A man born in September of 1846 by the name of Jasper Newton Daniel who called himself "Jack".

And today, *Jack Daniel's Sour Mash Tennessee Whiskey* is the best known American whiskey in the world.

notes:

1) just for golf fans, there's an old joke that goes, "the British open is such a great tournament, it's a shame they don't play it in the summer."

2) born in Inverness, Scotland, Doctor James C. "Jim" Crow (1789-1846) was the Scottish creator of the process for creating Bourbon whiskey. However, he is not the same Jim Crow after whom the discriminatory laws that were passed in the post Civil War South were named.

The Big Cat

On August 15th, 1947, The Union Jack, the flag that had represented Great Britain and had flown proudly over the British Empire was lowered for the final time at the Government House in New Delhi, and a new flag representing the finally independent Union of India was raised, thus ending over three centuries of British dominance on the sub-continent of Asia. It would not be the last colony to fall, but it would be the most significant since the loss of the American colonies in 1776.

The fall of India, which would later be followed by the fall of the French domination of Southeast Asia, was emblematic of a newly emerging political reality; that the old European powers had finally found the point where their reach exceeded their grasp; a turning point from which, in the not too distant future, the tables would be turned. The weak would become the strong and perhaps, the master would become the servant.

I mention all of this because, in the first decade of <u>this</u> century, Great Britain would also lose one of the symbols of its commercial and industrial dominance of the globe, embodied in the name of an automobile company that started with the most humble of beginnings, and even today still represents a great deal of what we collectively think of as British.

About the same time that Mohandas Gandhi was working for political reform in India, two motorcycle enthusiasts in England started a business that had absolutely nothing to do with politics or India but whose product would eventually symbolize a change of events that no one could possible imagine at the time. Their names were William Lyons and William Walmsley, both of Blackpool in Northern England.

By the end of the first World War, thanks mainly to its extensive use by the military, the motorcycle had become all the rage with the general public, and one of the accessories that people liked to add to their motorcycle was...the sidecar. The younger of the two Williams, William Lyons, bought a sidecar for his motorcycle from his neighbor William Walmsley, who was making them by hand in the garage of his parents' home. That transaction was the basis of an entrepreneurial relationship that would last for years as, over the next twelve months, the two would go into the sidecar business.

As an aside, sidecars are still made today, but you hardly ever see one. That's because enough people were killed in the fool things over the years that they took on the nickname, "widow-maker." As a former advertising executive, I can personally tell you that having your product known as a "widow-maker" is probably not the best marketing idea since the invention of sliced bread.

But that didn't stop the two Williams from trying. In 1922, they set up a company which they called the *Swallow Sidecar Company* and they were off and running. By 1927, the sidecar business was going so well that the pair decided to branch out into making automobiles. Well, sort of. They actually began making custom car bodies that they could put onto the chassis of other car-makers. The idea wasn't original with Lyons and Walmsley; it was actually the way that a lot of people tried to cash in on the car craze of the 1920's.

Evidently, Lyons and Walmsley were pretty good at makings <u>cars,</u> as well. They bought automobile chassis for their cars from the Austin Motor Car Company, which would eventually go on to make cars like the *Austin Healey*. Business was so good that in 1927, the two renamed their company, *The Swallow Coach-building Company*, dropping the "sidecar" reference altogether. These guys were on a roll.

By 1931, the company had secured contracts to produce both motors and chassis for what was about to be renamed as, *"SS Cars Limited"*. The *"SS"* was the brainchild of William Lyons who wanted to keep the initials of the original, <u>S</u>wallow <u>S</u>idecar.

Unfortunately, partnerships are difficult to maintain, and Lyon's partner, William Walmsley, didn't share his younger partner's vision of the future. Within a couple of years, Walmsley sold his interest in the business to Lyons.

Lyons' vision was to make better, faster and more expensive cars. Soon, appeared the SS I and the SSII; a pair of handsome cars that car enthusiasts loved, available in either a hardtop or convertible model.

Lyons would probably have kept the *SS* name forever except for the public relations problem that was created in the 1933 when Adolf Hitler became the Chancellor of Germany. When Hitler came to power, he brought along with him a gang of black-uniformed thugs that were known as the *Schutzstaffel* or *SS* for short, and somehow, the image of Hitler's stormtroopers was enough to force a name change for Lyons' car company.

The name that Lyons picked was based on a tremendously successful model that the company had introduced in 1935; a sleek low-slung beauty on four wheels that carried a hood ornament depicting a wild jungle cat, set in a pose as if it were about to pounce on something; a model that the company had decided to call: the *Jaguar*.

And from 1945 on, the company now known as *Jaguar* would produce some of the most distinctive cars in automobile history. Cars that emphasized what Bill Lyons had called, "grace, space and pace."

Now labeled with the simple designation, "XK", Jaguar set world-class standards for sports cars, first with the trend-setting XK 120 in 1949 and then in 1961 with what many auto enthusiasts still consider the most beautiful car ever built, the revolutionary Jaguar XKE.

Unfortunately, nothing lasts forever. Jaguar found itself in financial straits in the 1960's, and was soon being passed around like a bottle of rum on a slow boat to China. First, it merged into the *British Motor Company*, an offshoot of the old Austin Motors. Then, it was bought by an outfit called *Leyland*, a corporate hodgepodge which had to be bailed out by the British government. Then, it went public in a stock offering.

In 1999, Jaguar was sold to the Ford Motor Company. Unfortunately, Ford seemed to have a vision that everything it made should look like its best-selling Ford Taurus and sadly, the luster of the Jaguar seemed to fade as fast as the sun had set on the once invincible British Empire.

Finally, in 2008, Ford threw in the towel and sold the company to an Indian conglomerate that got its start making railroad locomotives just two years before England granted independence to India.

And that's the story of how an Indian manufacturing giant named, TaTa Motors, ended up owning the car company that had once been the pride of Great Britain; a company that started out making sidecars but is known the world over as...

Jaguar.

Nothing Runs Like It

The field of Economics is often referred to as the dismal science. The term was coined by the Scottish essayist, Thomas Carlyle, and was inspired by the writings of the Reverend Thomas Malthus whose *Essay on the Principle of Population* in 1798 warned of a world doomed to overpopulation, starvation and poverty as mankind struggled to feed a geometrically increasing number of people. Malthus' basic thesis was that food production simply could not keep up with population growth. At the time, the world's population was just under a billion. Of course, it should be noted that, ever the optimist, Malthus believed that war, pestilence and disease would keep the population in check from time to time; sort of the Malthusian version of seeing the glass half full. Pretty dismal stuff alright.

Fully two centuries later the world continues to thrive, but why? Certainly, there have been wars, famine, drought and the rest of it, but today the population has increased more than six-fold and relatively fewer people go to bed hungry now than in Malthus' day. And one of the reasons is that America, with its Great Plains, became the breadbasket of the world.

When we think of the Great Plains we are almost always reminded of the words of Katherine Lee Bates, the school teacher from Wellesley,

Massachusetts whose *America The Beautiful* spoke so eloquently of spacious skies and amber waves of grain.

But there was a time, just decades before Ms. Bates put pen to paper, when not a single stand of golden wheat grew in the vast prairie; a time when nothing but grassland covered the seemingly endless stretch from the Mississippi River to the purple mountain majesties of the Colorado Rockies.

The rolling wheat fields of America are, for the most part, the result of an invention by one man who made an improvement to a farm implement that had been in existence for well over five thousand years; an invention that came to be known as, "the plow that broke the Plains".

The plow itself is one of the greatest tools of all time. We take it for granted, but without it, the Grim Reaper would be knocking on the door and making Thomas Malthus look like a genius. The modern plow is an amazingly efficient device that simultaneously breaks the ground, turns it over, digs a trench, plants a seed, covers the seed and leaves a little channel to irrigate the whole thing.

Early plows date back about five thousand years, and they were pretty simple; get a big sharp stick, harness it to an ox and off you go. The ancient Greeks had a better idea than the big sharp stick. It was called the "crooked plow" because it had a *slanted* plane on it that helped turn over the soil. It was copied by the Romans and was pretty much the standard up until about the time of George Washington. It was better than a stick, but it is not the inspiration behind the plows that farmers use today. The forerunner of the modern plow was actually introduced to the western world by Dutch farmers, who imported it from China, where it had been used for a couple of centuries. And it is that Chinese plow, with its curved design, that flips soil so beautifully into the long lines or furrows in a freshly plowed field.

Speaking of furrows, here's an interesting bit of trivia. If you've ever wondered why an acre has the odd measurement of 43,560 square feet, here's the answer: an Ox can pull a plow about an eight of a mile in a single line or 'furrow' before it needs rest. That eight of a mile is called a *furlong*, literally a 'long furrow'. An average Ox can plow a field that is 66 feet wide by one furlong in a day. Do the math and you'll have an acre[1]...which is what one ox can plow in one day. Push your ox much harder than that and you'll have to go down to the local Ox dealer and buy a new one.

Anyway, by the early 1800's the curved Chinese plow was all the rage, the first real improvement in farming since the Romans. Local blacksmiths made them by hand out of iron and they worked great in the sandy soils of the eastern part of the country. But as farmers moved west they soon discovered a new problem; the dense clay soils of the Great Plains. The problem was that iron is too, let's say "sticky" for all that clay. The clay stuck to the iron plows and made them useless unless they were cleaned and re-cleaned constantly. In fact, they had to be cleaned every couple of yards. The work was so slow and frustrating that many new arrivals to the area simply gave up and went back east. When the going got tough, they got going...back to New Jersey. A lot of Native Americans probably wish they had <u>all</u> given up.

The solution came in 1837 when a young blacksmith from Middlebury, Vermont by the name of John Deere fashioned a new plow, this time made of polished steel. Deere got the idea, as a youth, from polishing steel needles to help them glide through leather more easily, and later he applied the concept to the farm implements he made in his blacksmith shop. And, it turns out, that a properly curved, <u>polished steel</u> blade on a plow will actually clean itself, and the chore of turning the soil, one furlong at a time, could proceed with little delay.

The invention was so successful that over 10,000 of the so-called "self polishers" had been sold before 1850. This single invention was the beginning of a company, and an agricultural revolution that turned the

North American grassland into the most efficient producer of wheat in the world.

A simple improvement of the Chinese plow, devised by an American blacksmith that changed the world.

Today, the familiar Green and Yellow tractors, combines, harvesters and plows of...

Deere and Company

are an integral part of the very landscape the company helped to transform over 170 years ago. After all as the company ads proudly proclaim, *"nothing runs like a Deere."*

footnote:

1) a mile is 5,280 feet; an eight of a mile (or furlong) is 660 feet; 660ft x 66 rows works out to 43,560 square feet, which is why an acre is such a weird number. Cool, huh?

Three Brothers and a Band-Aid

On September 8th, 1900, long before there were weather satellites, before there was ship to shore radio that could warn any of those on land of impending natural disasters forming at sea, as astonished weather observers watched their barometers fall to record low readings, a great storm rose out of the Gulf of Mexico and swept ashore over the city of Galveston on the southern coast of the State of Texas. It was the worst natural disaster in American history with conservative estimates of at least eight thousand lives lost.

In the wake of the storm, one of the companies that sent medical supplies to the area was a company that had been founded fifteen years earlier by three brothers in New Brunswick, New Jersey. The company would repeat the act of generosity in 1906 to aid victims of the Great San Francisco Earthquake and has been similarly generous for well over a century. Three quarters of a century later that same company would become the centerpiece of one of the most horrific crimes in American history; a crime that remains officially unsolved.

This maker of medical supplies was founded by Robert Wood Johnson and his two brothers, James and Edward. Johnson had been inspired after hearing a speech by the famous medical reformer, Joseph Lister, who for many years had advocated the practice of antiseptic surgical procedures.

Nowadays, we take it for granted that doctors will practice the most stringent antiseptic routine prior to walking into an operating room, but up until about 1865, physicians routinely went from home to home, covered in bloody work clothes, often without bothering to wash their hands, thus contaminating each new patient with germs from the last patient.

It was the French scientist Louis Pasteur who proved the dangers of germs in the practice of medicine and, building on his work, Lister had devised a way for doctors to work in a sterile environment. And, yes, it is the same Joseph Lister for whom the mouthwash "Listerine" is named.

But that is just the beginning of the story.

Upon listening to a lecture by Joseph Lister, Robert Wood Johnson convinced his brothers to go into business making sterile surgical bandages mainly for use in hospitals. It was an idea whose time had come. After enjoying early success, the brothers Johnson published a book entitled, *"Modern Methods of Antiseptic Wound Treatment."* It wasn't exactly a page burner, but it set the standard for operating room practices and without question saved thousands, if not millions, of lives.

Next on the brothers' winners list was a commercial first aid kit that is still made today, although with different packaging. It was originally designed for railway workers. Railroading has always been hazardous, but in 1888 if you worked on the railroad you were almost guaranteed to be injured on the job, and the brothers' first-aid kit became a mainstay of the industry.

In 1894, the company introduced a maternity kit to increase the safety of childbirth. One of the remnants of that product is still on the shelves today in the form of that sweet smelling baby powder that is found in nearly every household in the modern world.

But the brothers didn't stop there. In 1898, the company rolled out (so to speak) a line of dental floss made from unused surgical silk.

Endless other beneficial products have become part of the medicine chest including *Band-Aids* which were conceived by company employee, Earle Dickson, and introduced in 1920. In 1954, the company introduced its *"No More Tears"* formula of baby shampoo.

In 1987, *Accuvue* contact lenses became part of the greatly expanded lineup of consumer products which, by 1994, had grown to include the first cardio-vascular stent for heart patients.

But now for the tragic part of the story.

If you look at the history of the world, and America in particular, it seems that all too often we have been bruised by a certain loss of innocence. Aside from the twentieth century's horrors of war, that saw killing on a scale once thought unimaginable, the actions of single, warped individuals have all too often shattered the collective faith of millions.

The assassination of John F. Kennedy forever broke the hearts of a generation of Americans. The senseless rampage of the Manson Family in the late 1960's had Americans locking their doors in fear for their lives. The safety that we generally took for granted, had vanished.

In the world of pharmaceuticals, a bad batch of polio vaccine from Cutter Laboratories, in 1955, had unnerved parents already desperate to protect their children from the heartbreak of polio. Then came *Thalidomide* and the birth defects that followed. And while all of the drug-related disasters were tragic, they were accidental. No one had ever tampered with medicine at random.

Then something happened.

On the morning of September 29th, 1982, a twelve year old girl by the name of Mary Kellerman became the first victim of a mass murder after taking a dose of extra-strength *Tylenol* in the Chicago suburb of Elk Grove, Illinois. The Tylenol had been tainted with potassium cyanide, a monstrous act that would take the life of the twelve year old. It was the beginning of a nightmare that terrified the nation and remains officially unsolved to this day. Tylenol was produced by McNeil Consumer Health, a division of the corporation founded by the Johnson family nearly a hundred years earlier, and while the response to the crisis was swift and decisive, six more victims would fall at the hand of the unseen menace.

There was an arrest in the case, a man named James W. Lewis would eventually be convicted of trying to extort a million dollars out of Tylenol's parent company. Lewis would serve thirteen years in prison but would vehemently deny his guilt in the actual murders, although the FBI strongly felt it had the right man.

It was a senseless and depraved act that for a time cast an undeserved shadow on the name of one of the stellar companies in American business; a company whose list of consumer products is almost endless, everything from *Aveeno* to *Cortaid* to *Neutrogena* to *Rogaine* and *Bengay*, not to mention *Sudafed, Benadryl, Mylanta,* the aforementioned *Tylenol,* and last but not least, *Listerine.* A total of over fifty name brands in the consumer division alone.

It is a company whose distinctive Red Cross was actually trademarked prior to the founding of the American Red Cross, and whose logo, both organizations used interchangeably for nearly a century, until a legal dispute developed, in 2004, which has since been resolved.

The company, built from scratch, that first traded on the New York stock exchange in 1944, and trades under the symbol JNJ; a company known world wide as...*Johnson and Johnson.*

Sing Sing

The other evening I was watching *American Idol* on Fox television. And as I was watching, three things hit me at the same time:

Number one; some people have a tremendous amount of talent.

Number two; some people don't have much talent at all, and

Number three; a lack of talent never stopped anybody from trying to sing.

We love to sing. Singing is fun. It makes you feel good. We do it in the shower, we do around the house, and right up to the time that somebody looks over and stares at us, we love to do it in the car.

American Idol is not the first show of its kind. Before "Idol", there was of course, *The Gong Show*, and before that there was, *Ted Mac's Original Amateur Hour*, which actually got its inspiration from a radio program called, *The Major Bowes Amateur Hour*. Major Bowes' broadcast was pretty much the granddaddy of them all, and the name pretty much sums it up; a bunch of amateurs performed for about an hour on the radio, and if they were lucky they got to come back, week after week. One of the winners on that show, who eventually wound up becoming a regular on the show was a guy by the name of Frank Sinatra.

Now most people don't know it, but Frank Sinatra had a somewhat weak voice. He couldn't really belt out a tune. A great singer, no doubt, and sure, he could turn up the juice when he had too, but he was never going to make it in the opera. What made the careers of great pop singers like Frank Sinatra and Bing Crosby possible was an invention by a German-born American named Emile Berliner who, in 1876, invented the microphone. And it pretty much changed singing forever.

Before the microphone, you practically had to have a set of iron lungs to hit the back of the room. It's one of the reasons that opera was so successful until the turn of the century. But, after the microphone, all you needed was a pair of good speakers. You could say that the microphone made singing more democratic. It allowed the common man or woman to have a shot at being a star. Instead of being classically trained, new stars emerged who were barbers, in the case of Perry Como, or truck drivers in the case of Elvis Presley; Johnny Cash used to sell appliances before he walked into Sun Records one afternoon. And the list goes on. The microphone created pop music, which eventually evolved into Rock, Rap, Hip Hop and all the other genres we take for granted.

Okay, so much for the microphone. Here's a fun word....*Portmanteau*...it means a new word that comes from two old words. For example, *brunch* or *guesstimate*.

Now what does this have to do with American Idol or our passion for singing? Well, this is the story of another portmanteau, only this one come from a combination of two Japanese words which have grown together to become part of the American vocabulary.

The two Japanese words are: *Karano* and *Okesutora*. Which, roughly translated, mean *empty* or *missing orchestra*.

That's pretty much where we're headed. But, for now, let's take a little journey into the past; into the city of Kobe in Japan and an entertainer-slash-inventor by the name of Daisuke Inoue. Now if you've never heard of Inoue, don't worry, you're not alone. Although several years ago, *Time* magazine named him as being among the 100 most influential Asians of the twentieth century.

Daisuke Inoue was a musician, well of sorts. He started his career playing the drums when he was still in high school, banging on a set of drums that his parents undoubtedly regretted allowing in the home. Most parents do. Drums work out of great if your kid turns out to be Mick Fleetwood or Ringo Starr, but, for the most part, they're just a waste of money that keep you awake at night. From my personal experience, young people with drums don't need any sleep.

Anyway, after high school, Inoue started a band that played lounges in the Kobe area. None of the band members could sing worth a hoot, but that didn't make any difference; because the group had an unusual marketing angle. Instead of doing the singing, they just played the background music and let members of the audience get up on stage to bring their own magic to the songs; sort of a nightly lounge version of American Idol. As you can imagine, most of it, was pretty awful, but that didn't stop anybody from giving it the old college try.

By the late 1960's, Inoue and his band started to develop a following, and the story goes that one day a Japaneses businessman asked Inoue to travel with him to provide background music, so that the businessman could sing on stage when traveling. Because of prior commitments, Inoue had to decline, but he came up with the next best thing. He and the band pre-recorded a set of instrumentals on a cassette tape that the businessman could take with him and use to entertain co-workers and other victims while on the road.

The idea was a smash success, and a light bulb went off in Inoue's head. Why not build a machine with dozens or even hundreds of popular pre-recorded songs on cassette tape, all without the vocals... instrumental versions only. And, voila! ***Karaoke*** was born!

Now, in all fairness, people had been singing along with instrumentals for decades, but nobody had ever thought of making a machine that was <u>dedicated</u> to the purpose. And it was the Karaoke <u>machine</u> that Inoue invented. By 1971, he was leasing machines to bars all over Japan and the Philippines. It seemed like such an obvious idea to Inoue that he never bothered to patent the thing, and so missed out on millions of dollars he could have received from royalties.

Now, of course, Karaoke is just about everywhere. Karaoke clubs, Karaoke nights, Karaoke meet-up groups. It's a twenty-five billion dollar business that has probably sold more beer than the wet T-shirt contest, and the bar owner doesn't have to wring out the mop out at the end of the night.

And that's the story of how the microphone, a cassette tape and a little imagination from a Japanese drummer named Daisuke Inoue, combined to create an institution that allows anybody to get up on stage and sing his or her fool head off regardless of whether or not they have a lick of talent.

Since Inoue's machine took the place of the missing orchestra, he called it *Karano Okesutora or Kara Oke* for short...what we know as...

Karaoke.

The Battle Creek Boys

One of the fascinating facts about human behavior is that we tend to be driven by the calendar. The annual rituals that are governed by various dates are truly amazing. Of course, some are quite sensible; for example, it only makes sense to plant crops in the spring and harvest them in the fall. But that kind of behavior would go on regardless of any arbitrary date on a calendar. Even the dumbest caveman would eventually notice that all the snow had melted and the leaves had turned green. It's pretty hard to overlook the seasonal changes in nature.

Then again, take the annual ritual of the New Year's resolution. It is driven purely by the fact that there is, in fact, a New Year's Day; a simple landmark on the calendar. Every year, at about the same time, most of us resolve to get a fresh start on our lives, and for a huge number of people, we make what turns out to be a doomed promise to lose weight, eat healthier foods and generally start living the clean life.

With that in mind, our story today takes a look at the health food industry to see where all this business of losing weight and healthy eating got its start.

Of course, nowadays the weight-loss landscape is populated by companies like Jenny Craig, Judy Singer, NutriSystem, Weight Watchers and about a million wannabees all claiming to do the same thing; help us over-eaters lose weight; tons of it every year. In fact, if you add up all the pounds people have lost over the years…it's a miracle that anybody is still here. Erma Bombeck used to joke that in twenty years of dieting she had lost over a thousand pounds.

Nonetheless, dieting and healthy eating are here to stay, and undoubtedly for good reason, as Americans really have developed a weight problem.

But who would have ever thought that the serious business of healthy eating would eventually give birth to such caloric delights as Pop Tarts, Cheese-Its, and Keebler Cookies? Seems like something of a contradiction, although for legal reasons, I'm certainly not suggesting that any of those things are bad for you.

That said, let's begin our journey, and to do that, we have to go to church; a brand new Church, well new at the time, in the southern part of the state of Michigan, located between Detroit and Kalamazoo in a little town called Battle Creek, home to a movement known as the Seventh Day Adventists.

The Seventh-day Adventist church was formed in 1863. It differs from other Christian denominations in that it observes the Sabbath on Saturday, in the Jewish tradition and also adheres to the Kosher laws of the book of Leviticus; that certain foods should not be eaten, such things as pork, shellfish and other foods that are deemed to be unclean.

Consequently, they advocate a vegetarian diet and frown on the use of alcohol, tobacco and caffeine.

In 1866, church members established something called the Western Health Reform Institute, in Battle Creek, which encouraged its followers to eat a diet of clean, healthy, natural foods, and to exercise, get plenty of sun and enjoy the benefits of a healthy life. By all accounts, the Battle Creek facility, was enormously successful; so successful, in fact, that in 1878 the entire facility was re-built from the ground up and given a new name; the Battle Creek *Sanitarium*. By the way, up until then, the word Sanitarium didn't exist. It was the invention of the new superintendent, who changed the spelling of the word Sana**tor**ium.

And the name of that new superintendent was, John Harvey Kellogg, the same Kellogg that's probably sitting in your kitchen cupboard. But if you think that's the end of the story, sit back and have another spoonful of Frosted Flakes, because we're just getting started.

The Battle Creek Sanitarium developed quite a following, starting with just over a hundred patrons in the early days and boasting over seven thousand shortly after the turn of the century. The diet at the Sanitarium consisted largely of whole grain cereals as a source of carbohydrates and a minimal amount of protein. Sort of the opposite of what we would call the Atkins Diet today.

While John Harvey Kellogg was an excellent administrator, as the success of the Battle Creek Sanitarium will attest, he was not the business-savvy brains of the operation. That honor falls to John Harvey's little brother, Will, or Will Keith Kellogg to be more exact.

Young Will left his business selling brooms all over the Midwest to join his older brother in Battle Creek and after a few years of great success, the two of them created something that had never been seen, or eaten before. Something that changed the American dietary landscape forever. It was...the corn flake. Will and John made them by the millions, and people loved them. They ate 'em up!

The Kellogg brothers and their flaked cereals enjoyed great success, and the Battle Creek "San", as it came to be known, became a destination resort for some of America's most prominent citizens, including Mary Todd Lincoln, J.C. Penny, Henry Ford, President Warren Harding, Amelia Earhart, Johnny Weissmuller (who went onto star in the Tarzan movies) and a host of others who loved the taste of the crunchy breakfast morsels created by the Kellogg brothers. And, should anyone ask, John Harvey took great delight in showing just how the corn flakes were made, even though brother Will thought the idea should be kept secret because of its obvious commercial potential.

John Harvey would have been wise to listen to his younger brother, because one of the visitors to the Sanitarium was a gentleman by the name of Charles William "C.W." Post, who had traveled to the "San" for his ailing health. When Post learned how the flaking process worked, he had a bright idea; he could start a breakfast cereal company. And that's just what he did, in 1895.

Post's first product, was something called *Postum*, named after himself. It was a warm grain <u>beverage</u> that he envisioned as a coffee substitute. Postum never really caught on, but C.W. wasn't discouraged. He went on to create a genuine best seller; something that had the crunch of nuts and smelled like grapes as it was being cooked...at least that's what Post thought it smelled like...and so he called it...*Grape Nuts*.

Next on the list was something made from the Kellogg brothers' flaking process. It was originally called Elija's Manna. If you've never had a bowl, don't worry, you're not alone. That's because it was re-named soon after its creation and today we know it as, *Post Toasties*.

The irony of the story is that W.K. Kellogg got into the cereal business only **after** seeing the success that Post had enjoyed using the Kelloggs' idea and in 1906, Will founded The Battle Creek Toasted Corn Flake Company. Later, Will changed the name to *The Kellogg Company*, added a little sugar to those Corn Flakes and the next thing you know, you had Tony the Tiger telling you...they're great!

Both companies, of course, have enjoyed monumental success over the years. Kellogg's still retains its original name, while *Post Cereals* would eventually merge into the food giant, *General Mills*, but is now owned by *RalCorp* which used to call itself *Ralston Purina*. My how things change.

And that's the story of two brothers named **Kellogg**, who served a bowl of corn flakes to a man named, C.W. ***Post***...who turned the idea into a business that forever changed the menu of the American breakfast.

Picture This

The other day I saw a sign for "One Hour Photo Processing" and I wondered how long it would be before film cameras would become a thing of the past in our increasingly digital world. The last batch of the legendary Kodachrome, the stuff that Paul Simon wrote a song about, was produced in June of 2009. The old makes way for the new, and that is the way of the world.

Nowadays, photography is commonplace; even our phones have cameras in them, but before 1825, it had never happened. What we take for granted today was in many ways, accidental. A series of accidents that literally changed the world.

Today's story is about a little gold and silver, a little nitrogen, a search for a new kind of explosive and how they all eventually combined to make their way into the name of a company that is synonymous with...photography.

First, a short lesson on Nitrogen. Nitrogen is really great for making explosives. That's because it always wants to get back into the atmosphere, which is mostly made of...Nitrogen. When you combine nitrogen with just about anything else, it always wants to break loose, real fast, so fast that, with just a little nudge, it explodes. That's why gunpowder contains potassium Nitrate, a fertilizer bomb is made of ammonium **Nitrate**, and why **nitro**-glycerine is used in Dynamite. Nitrogen is... "The bomb."

So much for our chemistry lesson, now let's take a look at gold and silver. In the 13th century, the Catholic Bishop of Cologne, a man called, Albertus Magnus, believed that science and theology could live together in harmony. Pretty radical idea at the time, but it led him to fiddle with all sorts of chemical compounds. He basically invented nitric acid, which is full of nitrogen. He made the nitric acid by heating up potash, which is mentioned in the Book of Jeremiah in the Old Testament. (You really can mix science and religion.) Anyway, the good Bishop thought it might be fun to pour a little of his nitric acid onto some gold nuggets. That's because gold often has silver mixed in with it and Albertus wanted to see if the acid would separate the silver from the gold, and to his own amazement, it did. The experiment left two things in the bowl; a chunk of gold and a slimy liquid that would turn your skin black. We'll come back to that later.

Okay, now for the explosives. About 500 years later, scientists were still trying to figure out what kind of mischief they could get into with Nitric Acid and all that nitrogen that was locked inside.

In 1846, a German-Swiss chemist named Christian Schoenbein was working around the house and knocked over a jar of nitric acid onto the kitchen table. I bet that made a pretty big hit with the Mrs.. Anyway, the good Dr. Schoenbein grabs a cotton apron, soaks ups the acid and hangs the whole thing up to dry, which it does. And <u>when</u> it does...it explodes. Schoenbein had accidentally invented something called, "gun-cotton."

Unfortunately, gun-cotton exploded a little <u>too easily</u>, so chemists looked for ways to make it less volatile, after all, something that explodes when you hang it out to dry isn't much good for anything except maybe blowing up clotheslines. Anyway, after a lot of experiments and presumably a lot of kitchen tables, somebody poured sulfuric acid on a sheet of gun-cotton and when they did, two things happened; the cotton stopped exploding, and the sheet turned into a wafer-thin kind of plastic they called "celluloid." Today we call it film.

Okay, now for the One-hour photos.

Remember that slimy liquid that turned your skin black? That liquid is called silver nitrate, one of whose chemical properties is that it turns dark whenever it's exposed to sunlight.

Well, in 1825, a Frenchman named Joseph Niepce had the crazy idea that if the silver nitrate would react to light he could smear some of the stuff on a piece of tin, focus an image on it, and capture the image on the silver nitrate. And, to his amazement, his idea worked! Black and white photography was born. It's a little more complicated than that, but it's pretty close. Niepce was a real smart guy. He also invented the internal combustion engine, but that's another story.

Anyway, Niepce and a partner named, Louis Daguerre, eventually worked out a system to make photographs. Well, Louis did most of the work, since Niepce died along the way, which is why early photography was called Daguerreotype instead of Niepce-type. To take a picture, you smeared a chemical solution on a glass plate, stuck it in a camera, and let the light in. The only problem was that if the chemicals on the plate dried out, the process wouldn't work, which meant you had about an hour to turn out a picture. That meant if you wanted to be a photographer you pretty much had to carry a complete chemistry lab with you. Matthew Brady, the famous Civil War photographer, hauled an entire lab around with him in the back of a covered wagon. What a hassle!

Anyway, in the 1870's, along came a guy with a great idea by the name of George Eastman who did two things: first he came up with a way to make photographic plates that were already dry. You could take as long as you wanted to develop your pictures. That took the hassle out of photography. In 1881 Eastman set up a company called the *Eastman*

Dry Plate Company. And then, he had a <u>really</u> brilliant idea; he figured out how to get his dry chemicals onto that cellulose film that came from gun-cotton.

And since that "film" could be rolled-up on a spool, anybody could take your pictures, roll them up, put them in an envelope and mail them back to the Eastman lab to be developed; Eastman even made a little camera that practically did it all for you. As the ads said, "you press the button and we do the rest."

After a while, Eastman decided he needed a new name for his company. So, he and his mother worked on creating a brand new word, something unique and easy to remember, that had to have the letter K in it; because George thought "K" added power to a word. Well, if one K was good, two K's had to be perfect. Just slip a "D" in the middle and we're in business.

I don't know if they scribbled letters on napkins all afternoon or just got out the old "Scrabble Board" (I'm just kidding, Scrabble came along in 1938) but in 1892, using a brand new word, the old company was renamed, and would go on to become the biggest maker of photographic film in the world.

And that's how a little bit of silver, a spilled beaker of nitric acid, a cotton apron, two K's and a D combined to make a little company called...

Eastman <u>Kodak.</u>

The Shipping News

Let's start with a question. What do you, most of your friends, Brooke Shields, Betty Grable, Tina Turner, River Dance King Michael Flatley, AIG and the slave trade all have in common?

The simple answer is, insurance. Almost everybody has it. And the more you have to lose, the more insurance you probably own.

But where did the idea of insurance come from? How long has it been around?

While the modern form of insurance, with all the fine print, special riders and seemingly endless complexities has been around for about three hundred years, the origins are ancient.

The basic concept of insurance is to insure against loss, and that is how it got its start; mostly in the import and export business dating all the way back to the code of Hammurabi. If you're a little unsure of the date, Historians put the reign of Hammurabi at about 1750 B.C. The way insurance worked, way back when, was quite simple.

Let's say that it's 3,000 years ago when the center of the civilized world was built up on the shores of the Mediterranean Sea. I'm leaving the Chinese out here, because I'm a westerner and it's my story. Your occupation is that of a merchant. You buy goods from one part of the Mediterranean, and have a boat owner ship them over the perilous ocean so that you can sell your goods somewhere else. Just as we do today.

Back then, as now, most merchants had to borrow the money from a banker to buy their goods and have them shipped. But how would you pay back the bank, if the ship with all your goods on it, sank? I mean, even the Titanic sank, and it was probably built better than some Egyptian barge that was constructed before anybody had ever heard of King Tut. The way you <u>insured</u> your cargo was to pay the banker a *premium*. That premium would allow you to cancel your debt to the bank if all your goods went down to the bottom of the Ocean with Neptune or Poseidon or whichever of the gods of the sea was running the show at the time. That was the start of "insurance" which still refers to the payments you make as "premiums."

Over time, lenders got to be pretty savvy about collecting those premiums. They started suggesting that merchants spread their cargoes over several ships, so that if one was lost it wouldn't be a complete disaster. They started asking for higher premiums if the sea lanes were full of pirates or other raiders. Trade had become so important, economically, that the ruling city-states routinely escorted ocean cargo transports for their protection.

The Romans were particularly adept at keeping the sea lanes open from the ever-raiding Carthaginians, who made so much trouble that finally, in the year 149 BC, Rome sacked Carthage and sowed its land with salt, so that nothing would grow there for a hundred years. The Romans didn't mess around.

Okay, let's fast forward to the 1600's. The Romans were gone, The Carthaginians were gone, having never acquired a taste for salty food, and Great Britain was the supreme ruler of the sea. They had to be. They live on an island and not much grows there. And the biggest sea port in the world was a little town on the river Thames, called London.

Now, if you've ever been to a seaport, you'll soon discover that sailors like to drink. They especially like hot drinks. Hot Toddy's, Hot Buttered Rum, Irish Coffee. They like their drinks hot because it's cooold out there on the ocean and once you get them bones cold, it's hard to warm 'em up. If you've ever seen the movie, *The Perfect Storm*, it looks like everybody in the town of Gloucester hangs out at a place called, The Crow's Nest, to warm up after a week on the Grand Banks or the Flemish Cap or wherever fishermen go to catch fish for the hungry landlubbers having dinner at Red Lobster.

In the year 1688, London was no exception, and one of the most popular hangouts in the city was a coffeehouse on Tower Street that was owned by a gentleman named, Edward Lloyd. Lloyd not only served the usual fare of hot beverages to his patrons, but his shop also became a principal source of shipping news. Lloyd would post the schedules of ships, arriving and departing and would occasionally have to post news of any ships that were lost at sea.

Thus, Edward Lloyd's coffeehouse became something of an information hub. They didn't have Wi-Fi or the internet back then, but all that timely information had a very special appeal, not only to merchants and sailors, but also to a very select group of businessmen; the money-men who insured the cargoes that sailed the high seas. After a while, so many insurance people began to congregate at Edward Lloyd's coffeehouse that they began writing insurance policies on the spot, and if you didn't hang out at Lloyd's, you probably missed the boat...so to speak.

Anyway, in 1774, long after Edward Lloyd had passed away, what by now was a vast community of insurance underwriters, started congregating at a place called, The Royal Exchange; it's sort of the British equivalent to Wall Street, and they founded an insurance exchange that they called, *The Society of Lloyd's*, in honor of Edward Lloyd and his coffee shop. Contrary to common belief, the *Society* is not an actual insurance company, but, rather, a collection of companies and private investors who all happen to be in the same business. They insure just about everything. One blemish on their reputation stems from the fact that prior to the American Civil War, they insured cargoes of slaves from west Africa. It was standard practice at the time since, tragically, slaves were considered property. It was a practice that, came to an end with the abolition of slavery in America.

Now to get back to the trivia question from the beginning of the story. What do Brooke Shields, Betty Grable, Tina Turner and Michael Flatley all have in common? They all either have or had their <u>legs</u> insured by the *Society of Lloyd's*...or what we know as...

Lloyd's of London.

All In The Family

Remember the movie, *Bob and Carol and Ted and Alice*? I remember the title, but couldn't tell you anything about the movie. As I recall, it was pretty racy stuff at the time, and really has nothing to do with today's story, except that today's story is full of different names as well, but nowhere near as racy.

It's about as all-American as apple pie and the girl next door. I call it the story of Ruth and Kenneth and Barbara and Elliot and Harold and Lilli, and it will take us from a picture frame company to not only one of the largest toy companies in the world, but unquestionably the most successful doll-maker in history.

Now speaking of dolls, I have to admit that I don't know much, if anything about them, and I'm not going to apologize for it. But dolls and doll collecting are a big business. You'll find books on collectible dolls, rare dolls, Chinese and Japanese dolls. Doll houses, doll house furniture. Dolls are a big deal.

The crème de la crème of the commercial dolls is something called the Madame Alexander Collection. They have all sorts of dolls including their *Gone With the Wind* collection; You can get a Rhett Butler and a

Scarlett O'hara, and the pair will set you back about five hundred dollars. I don't know why they cost so much and, "frankly my dear I don't give a"....well you know. For that kind of money, you can probably get a room full of Barbie and Ken dolls, along with Barbie's Corvette and the Winnebago. My daughter had both.

Which brings us to a doll named Lilli. Lilli was a cartoon creation who first appeared in a German tabloid newspaper, called *Die Bild-Zeitung* in 1953. She was the creation of a cartoonist by the name of, Reinhard Beuthein. The newspaper needed to fill some blank space in its upcoming issue and Reinhard got the assignment. His first drawing was of a traditional baby doll, but his editor wasn't wild about it, so he went back to the drawing board, literally. His next effort started something really big. It was an adult looking doll, a thin and curvy young woman in her late teens or early twenties with a pony tail and he called her, Lilli. Lilli became so popular as a cartoon strip character that, soon, a German toymaker started making the *Bild-Lilli* doll.

Now, enter a woman by the name of Ruth Handler. Back in 1945, Ruth Handler and her husband Elliot had formed a company with a man named Harold Matson, whose principal business was the making of picture frames. The company had done well over the years making picture frames, but something bothered owner Elliot Handler; all those picture frames created a heck of a lot of left-over wood pieces and so, not being one to just throw all that wood into the dumpster, he started making...doll houses and doll house furniture, and that turned out to be a very successful enterprise. The Handlers and their partner Harold Matson were now on their way to being in the toy business.

In 1955, the company got a real boost when it started advertising toys on the brand-new Mickey Mouse Club. One of its best sellers was something called the *Burp Gun*. It was a machine gun that fired caps. I had one as a kid. Made a lot of noise and got the whole house to smell like gunpowder. My parents were divorced shortly thereafter. Not sure if there's a connection.

Anyway, Ruth Handler got the idea to produce a doll collection, in part to amuse her daughter, Barbara; and that's when she discovered the German doll named, you guessed it...Lilli. Ruth met Lilli on a trip to Europe in 1956, gave one to her daughter and brought back a dozen or so to pass around at company headquarters. Nobody was impressed; there's no hope for a prophet in his...or her own land. But, by 1959, Ruth prevailed and with a few revisions re-created Lilli into a doll named after her young daughter, who just happened to be named, *Barbie*. A couple of years later Barbie got a boyfriend who just happened to be named after the Handler's other child...a boy named, Ken. Over the years, Barbie...and Ken...have added a Corvette, a Winnebago, and a jet plane to their long list of accessories which includes endless lines of clothing and enough shoes to make Imelda Marcos green with envy.

Barbie and Ken, and later Skipper and Scooter became the foundation of a company that gave birth to such blockbusters as *Chatty Cathy*, the *Rock 'em Sock 'em Robots, Pictionary*, the *Lie Detector* game, *Matchbox* Cars and Trucks, the *Pound Puppies*, and the *Cabbage Patch Kids* to name just a few.

They all belong to the American company that was named after two of its founders, Harold "Matt" Matson and Elliot Handler, who, back in 1945, combined their names Matt and Elliot and ended up with a little company called...

Mattel.

Daddy's Little Girl

By all accounts, the Paris Universal Exposition (or World's Fair) of 1889 was one of the great triumphs of the late 19th century. It was a marvel of entertainment and scientific achievement. Buffalo Bill Cody had recruited Annie Oakley to dazzle audiences with her sharpshooting skills; an audience that would include the future King Edward VII of England, artists Paul Cezanne and Vincent Van Gogh and the American inventor, Thomas Edison.

At the entrance to the fair stood the as yet unfinished Eiffel Tower. Within the grounds of the fair, stood an exhibit called the Gallery of Machines. At nearly 365 feet in length, the Gallery was home to the largest enclosed space on the planet at the time.

It was an architectural wonder that housed, among other things, a three-wheeled contraption that had almost never been seen before. It was the world's first gasoline-powered horseless carriage, and while it was considered a novelty at the time, it would mark the unofficial beginning of an industry that would forever change the world. The vehicle was called, *the Benz Patent Motorwagen*, so named after its creator,

Karl Benz, a German engineer who had been granted a patent for the contraption in 1886.

Benz was fortunate to have secured the patent, because two other engineers, Gottlieb Daimler and Wilhelm Maybach, also Germans, had been working independently on the same idea. The Benz *MotorWagen* was a composite of other devices cobbled together to create something new. Most of the components; the gasoline engine, the carburetor, the tiller for steering, had been used in other applications, but Benz had combined them into a single unit and that's why he got the patent for the automobile.

The first *"Benz"* made its public debut with a less than promising performance; it crashed into a wall in front of a crowd of spectators who had come to see something they surely thought was a mere passing fad. After all, nothing was going to replace the horse and buggy.

But Benz was not dismayed. He kept at it and soon after came out with an improved model, which was easier to steer and stop as well. I'm no engineer, but from personal experience I can attest to the fact that steering and stopping are essential ingredients in automobile design.

Now, just in case you haven't been keeping up with current events, it turns out that the people who bet on <u>cars</u> made a lot more money than the people who bet on <u>horses</u>. By the first part of the twentieth century, everybody and his uncle was making cars and Karl Benz was doing a lively business. In America, the Duryea bothers were first on the scene, they were soon followed by Ransom Eli Olds, whose company went on to build Oldsmobiles. Henry Ford was a latecomer to the business, but used the power of mass production to give the automobile the foothold that it has never lost.

Back in Germany, Maybach and Daimler were in the business as well, turning out cars to compete with Karl Benz and numerous other rivals, and it was their company, not Benz's that would become the dominant player in Germany's automobile industry. By the mid 1920's, with a seemingly endless list of rivals, it became obvious that sooner or later many would either go broke or have to merge with one another and, predictably, the industry underwent a major consolidation. In America, William Durant had created General Motors out of half a dozen competitors and in Germany, rivals Daimler and Benz merged to compete with four companies that had merged themselves under the name, *Auto Union*, which now are part of the company that includes *Porsche*, *Audi* and *Volkswagen*.

As far as corporate identity goes, Daimler always had the upper hand in the merger of Benz and Daimler, which is why the company is now simply called, *Daimler AG*.

Now, a lot of owners like to refer to their car as a Benz, but...nobody ever refers to their car as a Daimler. What they refer to marks the final chapter in the storied history of this legendary company.

The early model of the Daimler cars was called, the *Phoenix*, and it was an engineering marvel. Fast and reliable, the Daimler Phoenix was the favorite of all who could afford it; a testament to the quality and the design of the two engineers, Daimler and Maybach, who had created it. But, in the real world, engineers don't sell things; salespeople do.

Almost since its inception, one of Daimler's principal champions was a successful Austrian businessman and entrepreneur named, Emil Jellenik. Always quick to see an opportunity, Jellenik served not only as a customer but also as something as a salesman for the Daimler Company, selling cars to his wealthy friends. Jellenik was also a racing enthusiast and, as such, he pushed Daimler to build racing cars. Of course, at the turn of the century the speeds were pretty slow in comparison to the two hundred-plus miles per hour that is regularly seen at the track nowadays. Back then, forty miles per hour was considered fast and furious.

Emil Jellenik raced the Daimler cars throughout Europe with great success. It was a fact that helped establish Daimler's reputation for building cars that were both fast and reliable. But, when he raced, he did so under a pseudonym, and it is that pseudonym by which most of us refer to the signature marque of the company whose hood ornament is the unmistakable three-pointed star.

Jellenik took his daughter's name as his racing monicker, and would one day remark that he was probably the only father who had ever done so. It is a name that comes from the Spanish, *Our Lady of Mercy*, which explains why the signature name of the Daimler Motor Company that merged with the Benz Motor Company bears the name of Emil Jellenik's eleven year-old daughter...

Mercedes.

The Landlord's Game

Have you ever dreamed of being a real estate tycoon? A millionaire, living the life of luxury collecting rents from all sorts of people; being a Donald Trump, owning some of the most prestigious properties in the world, or just being a slumlord, shaking down the 'po' folks for the monthly rent check. If you said "yes" then you're not alone, because you'd be a member of a vast community that has done just that in a fantasy game that has been played in countries all over the world. Because, this is the story of the world's most famous <u>board</u> <u>game</u>.

First, a little history. The oldest known board game was played by the Egyptians about fifty-five hundred years ago. It was called, senet; something that archeologists figured out by deciphering ancient Hieroglyphics. They discovered the game because a picture of people playing senet was found in the tomb of a guy named, Merknera. We don't know much about Merknera, but apparently the game of senet was popular enough to merit a painting inside his tomb. If you're a fan of the popular TV series *Lost*, in one of the episodes, a couple of kids discover what appears to be a version of the ancient senet game while digging around on the beach.

Okay, so let's talk about some other board games. I mentioned senet, which you can actually buy at game stores. Nobody really knows how the Egyptians played it. Somebody had to make up the rules for modern players. The next oldest game is *backgammon*, which is about five thousand years old, followed by the Indian game of, *Pachisi*, the Chinese game of *Go*, then finally by *chess* which was also invented in India about 500 AD. Checkers, by the way, in its modern version, comes *after* chess. I'm talking, of course about checkers the game, and not the Nixon family's little dog.

Anyway, all of the ancient games can be fun if you're into that sort of thing, but they aren't generally considered a barrel of laughs, and they're usually limited to just two players at a time; great for old men at the park, but definitely a party killer.

Now, let's fast-forward to the year 1883, when a sixteen year-old by the name of George Parker invented a board game that he called, *Banking*. It was a theme game. There had been theme games before *Banking*, but generally they were meant to teach some kind of moral lesson. *Banking* was different. You borrowed money from the bank and then tried to get rich. No morality intended, and it made the teen age Parker about a hundred dollars profit all tolled. It wouldn't be the last game he invented, nor would it be the most popular, but it would be the start of a game-making empire that would change the way Americans and people from all over the world would spend their family time together.

If we were to take a poll of popular board games, most people would probably think of something like *Monopoly* or *Risk* or *Clue*. There's a game called, *Sorry,* that debuted around 1930. It's an Americanized version of Pachisi with a clever name since the word "Sorry" is really a misspelled take-off on the name of India's traditional clothing for women. While were at it, a company called Hasbro renamed, Pachisi, and trademarked it as, *Parcheesi.*

Now, the most famous commercial board game, which I rather offhandedly mentioned a second ago, was actually the brainchild of a woman named, Elizabeth Magie, who created a board game called, *The Landlord's Game,* as an educational tool for college students. The purpose was to demonstrate how landlords get rich and tenants stay poor paying rent all the time. Gee, do you really have to go to college to figure that out?

Anyway, Elizabeth Magie or 'Lizzie' as she preferred to be called, actually created something <u>new</u> in the game business. It's what's known as, the *continuous walk*; where players, using little tokens move round and round on the board covering the same territory over and over; unlike, say, chess, where the pieces can move just about every which way.

Around and around they went, the tokens that is, stopping on various properties and paying rent to the landlord. The properties were based on generic businesses. You could own and/or land on places like the neighborhood bakery, the power company or a railroad or two. There was a place to pay taxes, pick up a paycheck. It was pretty much like real life, which is why people seemed to like it. Everybody who played it thought it was a load of fun, so Lizzie created, the *Economic Game Company,* to produce and sell the *Landlord's Game.* But the Economic Game Company lacked the capital to make a go of it. So, in 1910, she approached our old friend George Parker, of the now successful Parker Brothers Game Company. And the result:, George Parker turned Lizzie down flat.

Not interested.

Thirteen years later, in 1923, the now <u>married</u> Lizzie Magie <u>Phillips</u> re-designed the game adding street names that were based on the City of Chicago; places like The Loop and Lakeshore Drive, and again she approached the Parker Brothers.

Not interested.

It seemed that *The Landlord's Game* was popular with everybody but the people in the game business. It was copied, literally, by hand and played on college campuses all over the mid-west. And, with each hand-drawn copy, often something new was introduced.

By the 1930's, a new variation of the game had been re-drawn by a man named Charles Darrow. Darrow included properties with names based on landmarks in Atlantic City, New Jersey and included four railroads, a water an an electric company, and a color scheme that identified properties that belonged together. Paydays were handled by a square called, *GO*, where you could pick up two hundred dollars and then face the gauntlet, once again, to see if you could make it around the board to another payday before you went broke.

In 1935, Charles Darrow took his game to the Parker Brothers with a new name.

Not interested.

So, he went to rival game maker, Milton Bradley. Not Interested. Too complicated. The people at the top sure know a winner when they see one, don't they?

Then, later in 1935, something changed. Apparently, the Brothers Parker turned up their hearing aids and discovered that everybody who had ever played the game loved it. The idea of being a landowner in the middle of the Great Depression had almost universal appeal. So, they invited Darrow back to their offices, made him an offer, and the rest is history.

The game with its now familiar Park Place, Boardwalk, Marvin Gardens and all the rest were purchased by the Parker Brothers under the new name that Charles Darrow had given to Lizzie Magie Philips' old *Landlord's Game*.

It's the most popular board game ever made. There's a British version where you can own places like *Trafalgar Square* and *Piccadilly*, and a

French version where you can own *The Champs Elysee* and *Rue de la Paix*...It's available in twenty-six languages and themes including Greek, Russian and Hebrew.

It's the game that the entire world knows as...*Monopoly*.

How Sweet It Is

I'm going to start today with a rather alarming statistic. According to the Surgeon General of the United States, as far back as 1999, sixty-one percent of the adults in the United States were either overweight or obese, and about fifteen percent of our kids are in the same category. And, the trouble is, that until you're about age 60, the longer you live, the fatter you get just naturally. Now, there are lots of causes, but the main sources are fat and sugars of all kinds.

With that in mind, today's story is for anyone who claims to have a sweet tooth; that craving for sweets of any kind, be it chocolate, caramel, taffy, toffee, cotton candy or any one of a thousand confections that make you feel good, add inches to the waistline, and unfortunately, cut years off our lives.

Because, this is the story of the history of <u>artificial</u> <u>sweeteners</u> and the company that started it all over a century ago.

One of the most interesting facts about artificial sweeteners is that the company that started the entire industry is one that you would never suspect of creating something that you would put into or onto food, and certainly not into your mouth. For the most part, the "Grand-daddy" of 'em all is best known as a producer of herbicides, the kinds of chemicals that you spray on your lawn to make the dandelions shrivel up and die. They also make the stuff that will kill your entire lawn; a weed killer called, *Roundup*.

Now, there are all sorts of sweeteners on the market today. Probably the best known is a chemical made from a, "dipeptide of aspartic acid and a methyl ester of phenylalanine." Just sounds good doesn't it. Well, the whiz kids on Madison Avenue didn't think so either, so they came up with something a little easier to pronounce, and they called it, *Aspartame*. For the most part, Aspartame is marketed under the brand name, *Nutrasweet*. There are a lot of critics of NutraSweet, and that could be the subject of a really serious paper, but since this is just for fun, the biggest complaint about Aspartame or NutraSweet is that it gives some people headaches, and it doesn't stay sweet if you use it for cooking. So much for NutraSweet brownies. Now, that's not the end of our story. Sit back, we're just getting started.

Sucralose is another sweetener that's available on the market, and it's sold under the brand name *Splenda*. Sucralose is actually made from real sugar with a little dash of chlorine thrown in among other things. The good news is, that little bit of chlorine in the mix makes the stuff about 600 times as sweet as real sugar. It's so sweet that they have to mix it in with granules of mostly inert stuff so it will look and feel like sugar. And, since it <u>is</u> made from sugar, you can bake with it. Of course, if you stuff your face with artificially sweetened brownies, you're still gonna get fat, because nobody ever lost weight by eating a pound of flour no matter how it was sweetened.

There are also a couple of natural sweeteners like *Stevia* and *Tagatose*. Tagatose has the most promise because it is a real sugar made from lactose. Unfortunately, Tagatose is on hold for now because of legal complications. The FDA approved the stuff in 2003, but it's a little unclear who owns the rights to make it.

Okay, so much for all the background, now let's get to the sweet spot, so to speak. The search for all of these different sweeteners was really brought about when, in the 1970's, the U.S. Food and Drug

Administration hit the panic button over a sweetener that everybody had used since the 1890's; a product called…*saccharine.* Now if you ask me, saccharine wasn't all that tasty. If you ever tried a diet soda in the 1960's, it tasted okay on the way down, but had an after taste that was down right nasty.

Saccharine was extremely popular, especially among health-conscious people, and even when suspicions arose about its safety, they were often dismissed. One of the advocates for saccharine was President Theodore Roosevelt. FDA historian, Suzanne White Junod, once quoted Roosevelt as saying that, "anybody who says saccharin is injurious is an idiot."

That may well have been Teddy Roosevelt's opinion, but in 1972, the U.S. Department of Agriculture went to court to try and have saccharine banned because it was linked to bladder cancer in laboratory rats. Saccharine was never banned, but Congress got into the act and soon after, it passed legislation requiring saccharine to carry a warning label. In 2001, the warning label was dropped after the FDA discovered that the rats they were using in the tests were unusually subject to bladder cancer themselves and the warning labels came off; but not before the sweetener industry had already filled the shelves with some of the previously mentioned alternative products.

Okay, so saccharine is the real story here. It's made from something called *Benzoic Sulfamide*, which comes from coal tar. The whole process is kicked off with something called, *Toluene*, which is a solvent used in the making of TNT, and will literally eat a hole in your driveway, mmmm, yummy!

Saccharine was discovered in 1878 by a chemist named, Constantin Fahlberg. He was conducting some experiments at Johns Hopkins University to find out what kinds of things you could make out of coal tar. Legend has it that he went home after a long day at the chemistry lab and as he was eating his supper he noticed that his fingers were unusually sweet. Evidently, Fahlberg didn't bother washing his hands before eating and I think it is also reasonable to conclude that he didn't always use a fork.

Anyway, a light bulb goes off in Fahlberg's head, and he figures he can make some dough out of this sweet stuff that must have come from the coal tar experiments. So, he gets to work and in 1885 he receives a patent on the process, trademarks the name, *Saccharine,* and soon starts to shop around for a buyer. He found one in Germany and for a time they held monopoly rights. Okay, were now at the sweet spot of the story.

Finally, we come to a chemist in St. Louis named, John Frances Queeny, and this is where our story will end, well, almost. If you've never heard of the Queeny Chemical and Saccharine Company, don't worry. There isn't one.

Queeny had been in the pharmaceutical business for about thirty years when he had the inspiration to produce Constantin Fahlberg's saccharine, commercially in the United States. With about $5,000 in start-up money, Queeny went into production and started a company that rather cleverly took the maiden name of his wife, Olga, whose father was a wealthy sugar producer in the West Indies…named, Emmanuel Mendes de…*Monsanto.*

It was the birth of a chemical giant that, today, is the third largest agricultural chemical company in the world.

The Last Late Fee

For better or for worse, one of the facts of the modern age is that we have an immense amount of leisure time. Of course, most people think they are worked to death, but compared to a century ago, we have it made. Take, for example, the late 1800's; when working-class men easily worked six, twelve-hour days every week, many never seeing the sun during the work week except in the summer. If it hadn't been for the biblical prohibition against working on the Sabbath, it's likely that our ancestors would have worked seven days a week. Thankfully, the influence of labor unions, better wages and a burgeoning middle class put pressure on employers to lighten the workload to what is now the standard 40 hour work week.

Throughout most of recorded history, leisure time didn't do you much good, because as soon as the sun went down there wasn't really much to do besides go to bed. Sure, people had candles and oil lamps, but let's face it; that's a lot like living in the dark ages. By the late 19th century all that had changed thanks, in part, to three inventions of Thomas Edison. One obvious invention was the incandescent light bulb, which was safer than gas lamps and lanterns, since they had a nasty tendency to either explode or catch the house on fire. Another was the phonograph, which while a far cry from today's standards still made for an enjoyable evening. And, last but not least, Thomas Edison invented...motion pictures. He wasn't the first with the idea, but he made the concept practical, and received a patent for it. And, ever since then, people have been flocking to the movies.

Now, except for one minor flaw, Edison's original stab at motion pictures was almost perfect. His only mistake was that he set the frame rate a bit too slow; just 16 frames per second; nowadays the standard is 24 frames per second. That's because 16 frames is not quite fast enough to fool the eye with the illusion of continuous motion, and as a result, early motion pictures tender to flicker, which is why movies are sometimes called *"flicks."*

Okay, let's fast forward about ninety years, when a company called JVC invented something called, VHS; it originally stood for *vertical helical scanning*, but JVC quickly called it the *Video Home System*. And it caught on like hot cakes. Now, instead of going to the movies, people could go to the movie store and rent a movie to watch at home. Which brings us to a guy named, Reed Hastings. If the name is unfamiliar, it is almost certain that you know the service that he created. It is used by millions of people every day who seek to fill their daily need to be entertained.

By almost any account, Reed Hastings is a guy who doesn't mind making waves; always searching for a better way to do things. There's a story about Mr. Hastings that he was allowed to leave the Marines and join the Peace Corps because he made too many, let's say, "suggestions," how the Marines could improve the way they did things. Apparently change comes slowly in the Corps. Semper Fi!

After the Peace Corps and graduation from Stanford, Hastings made a fortune with a software company called *Pure Soft* that fixed other people's software. I guess there's always room for improvement. Anyway, Reed Hastings sold *Pure Soft* and now found himself with a boatload of money and a lot of spare time. That's a powerful combination in the hands of the right person.

Two things Hastings liked to do were; go to the gym and rent movies, and thanks to VHS, movie rental stores were everywhere. What could be easier? Go to the store, rent a flick watch it for a couple of days and then return it.

It turns out that Reed Hastings and I share something in common. We both love the movie, *Apollo 13*, Ron Howard's spellbinder about the ill-fated moon-mission. I could watch it all day, and apparently so could Reed Hastings. He rented it one day, watched it a few times and then did what everybody has done at one time or another. He forgot to return it, and the clock started clicking.

Day after day, the late fees kept adding up. After six weeks the bill had grown to about forty dollars; not enough to break the bank of a millionaire software developer, but enough to get him to thinking that there must be a better way of doing things.

And what he came up with has completely transformed the movie rental business.

Hastings's bright idea was to change the business model for movie rentals and apply something different...something that came from the fitness center where he worked out. He realized that the gym doesn't care if you come in once a month or once a day....you can work out all day long for all they care. They just want a monthly rental fee for the use of the gym. And that's when the light bulb went off in Hastings's head; let people keep movies as long as they want; just return the old one in order to get a new one...all for a low monthly fee, and never again pay a late fee or go through the Saturday night scramble to get the VHS back to the movie store. And the rest is history.

Now, you could order your favorite movie on the internet, and a day later it would be in your mailbox waiting to be viewed to your heart's content. You could literally rent your flicks... over the net, which is why he called his company...

Netflix.

They Do Everything For Less

It is a fact that many, if not most, of the things that we take for granted were once things that inspired great awe and amazement when they were first invented. For example, just about everybody in America owns a car, and while we think of cars and trucks as commonplace, they are a remarkable assortment and combination of intricate machines, which themselves are an amazing assortment of individual parts, all created by the efforts of individual craftsmen or by machines that were fashioned by craftsmen.

Although we take the process for granted, the fabrication of all the gizmos and gadgets that comprise the most complex machines is something that is rather new to the history of mankind. A great deal of it was the brainchild of one man; one of the most remarkable characters in all of American History, a young man from New England by the name of Eli Whitney.

I don't know if they still teach anything about Whitney in the public schools. They may be too busy badmouthing capitalism and extolling the virtues of big government to get around to Whitney, but he is worth studying for a couple of reasons. The most often cited is his invention of the cotton gin, which had the effect of making cotton the greatest cash crop of the pre-Civil War South and arguably prolonged the institution of slavery.

But the truly seminal accomplishment of Eli Whitney, in part embodied in the cotton gin, was the concept of interchangeable parts. Whitney, having made little or no money from his cotton gin had a second great idea, and it changed the world forever. His idea was to create a new system of making rifles, or muskets if you will, for the U.S. Army. Prior to Whitney, guns, and for that matter just about everything else, were made by skilled craftsmen who would make each musket by hand. Literally, the lock, the stock and the barrel were all made by a single individual and then fitted together to create a complete firearm. The system had worked well enough for half a dozen centuries and nobody thought twice about it except, of course, Eli Whitney.

The problem with the old way of making guns was that if you needed a new, let's say, trigger, you couldn't just taken one from a gun that was no longer being used. That was unfortunate, because in the normal course of a battle, a lot of guns go unused since their owners are either wounded or killed.

Whitney's idea was to make gun parts to such precise specifications that any part could be used in any gun. It seems so obvious now, but then again, so does everything that we take for granted. To prove his point, Whitney put a big bag of gun parts together, dumped them on a table in front of President Thomas Jefferson and his advisers, and told them to assemble a musket from any part they wanted. (In those days, most people knew how to put guns together.) To their shock and amazement...it worked! Everyone was amazed...so amazed that Whitney landed a contract to make ten thousand muskets for the American Army.

The concept of <u>interchangeable parts</u> really caught on, so much so that it became known as *the American System*, and as much as anything else, it was the *system* that gave birth to the industrial age. It is really what makes things like the automobile, for example, possible.

The automobile is an amalgamation of thousands of interchangeable parts, without which the whole thing would either be impossible or every car would cost a million dollars. That's probably what the Defense Department pays for their cars.

Whether it's your air filter, your battery or your alternator, every part on your car comes in a box, with a part number and looks exactly like the one that it's replacing, which is a good thing because sooner or later, a lot of the parts on a car will need to be replaced. And, for better or for worse, that little fact of life is what gave birth to something else that we take for granted; the auto parts store, and that's the real subject of today's story.

Now, today, the commercial auto parts landscape is dotted with familiar names such as *Napa, O'Reilly, Checker, AutoZone*, and a host of others, not to mention the fact that any number of items are available at big box discounters and mail-order houses like *J.C.Whitney*. But, of course, that wasn't always the case.

One of the earliest of the companies still doing business today was started in Philadelphia by four enterprising young men who scraped together the vast sum of eight hundred dollars back in 1921. Their names were Emmanuel Rosenfeld, Maurice Strauss, Moe Radavitz and Graham Jackson. Moe Radavitz left the business after a couple of years, and that left only three.

The company enjoyed a stellar rise to success. By 1930, the partners had opened forty stores in the Philadelphia area using the name that they had taken from a manufacturer of an industrial polishing compound. It was a jar of something that had been left behind in their first storefront called, *Pep Valve Polishing Compound*. Try to say that three times in a hurry. The partners liked the name because it sounded kind of, well...Peppy! So they called their company, *Pep Auto Supplies*. The company got to be so well known that when somebody needed car parts in Philadelphia people would routinely say, "go down and see the boys at PEP Auto supplies." But that's not the end of the story.

It was in 1923, just two years into the business, when one of the partners, Maurice Strauss was in California scouting locations for a store on the west coast. He noticed a dress shop, run by three ladies who called their business, Minnie, Maude and Mable's and thought that adding the first names of the company founders would sound more customer-friendly. And while nobody ever heard of Emanuel, Maurice, and Graham's auto parts, the boys decided to use their nicknames of Manny, Moe and Jack (short for Jackson).

Business flourished until the advent of World War II when the auto business practically died and along with it the need for retail auto parts. But the *Pep Boys,* as they were now known, survived by selling other goods, mostly workman's clothing, to the thousands of employees being hired at America's wartime factories.

After the war, well, it was the golden age of the auto industry. Everybody wanted a car, and the auto parts business was back in high gear. The *Pep Boys* would go onto become one of the biggest companies of its kind, with over six thousand stores currently across the United States. And the little bobble-head figures of the three "boys"...they pretty much look like the founders...except that in 1990 the company took away Manny's cigar. Political correctness has no bounds.

And that's how Emanuel, Maurice and Graham took the name of Pep Valve Grinding Compound and turned it into something we know as...

The Pep Boys, Manny, Moe and Jack.

Ride Like The Wind

In Stephen King's short story and subsequent film, *The Shawshank Redemption*, the character, Brooks Hatlen, is released from prison as an old man in the 1960's only to discover that, to his horror, the world went and got itself in what he called, "a big damn hurry."

That seems to be the world that we have created for ourselves ever since the end of the dark ages, as information has become an increasingly sought-after commodity. Of course, today we can obtain information on just about anything in just a few seconds; a few keystrokes on the computer keyboard, a *Google* search and page after page of endless information is in front of us ready to be digested from top to bottom. The speed of all of it is breathtaking, and yet it is somehow taken for granted, this miracle of high tech communication.

But a century and a half ago, in the 1860's, nothing was taken for granted. New concepts of doing even the most mundane things like simply delivering the mail sparked the imagination. And one of those delivery systems remains the grist for storytellers and historians who have an interest in what was once the wild west. This is one of those stories.

On November 7, 1860, a lone rider and his horse left Fort Kearney, Nebraska Territory, on his way to Fort Churchill, Nevada Territory, with a pouch containing, among other things, the results of the 1860 election. Seven days and 17 hours later, a telegraph operator at Ft. Churchill relayed the message to San Francisco and voters in California learned that Abraham Lincoln had been elected the sixteenth President of the United States. It was the fastest time that breaking news had ever reached the west coast of the American empire.

If you ever take the time to drive to the summit of Lookout Mountain, just above the town of Golden, Colorado, you will find a grave site there that bears tribute to one of the greatest showmen of the nineteenth century; a man whose *Wild West Show* delighted audiences across the country and introduced, among others, a woman by the name of Annie Oakley to the American scene. That man was named, William F. Cody, but the world knows him as *Buffalo Bill*.

The story of William F. Cody begins with a newspaper ad. It read simply:

> "Wanted: Young, skinny, wiry fellows, not over eighteen. Must be expert riders, willing to risk death daily. Orphans preferred."

It was an ad placed in local papers in and around St. Joseph, Missouri by a company that had been created in 1849 by three entrepreneurs named, William H. Russel, Alexander Majors and William B. Wadell. The company had originally been formed as the Leavenworth and Pikes Peak Express Company, although nobody remembers it by that name. What people do remember is the service itself and the name that described that service.

Initially, some one hundred twenty riders, including Cody, were enlisted to do the following: carry a double mail pouch for about twenty miles on horseback and ride like the wind. Twenty miles was not the end of the journey for the <u>rider</u>; it was the end of the journey for the <u>horse</u>. Apparently, that's about as far as you can get a horse to gallop before it drops dead.

After twenty miles, the now breathless horse was exchanged for a new one, while the rider remained the same. On and on through day and night they rode. Through heat and cold, and rain and snow, across hostile Indian country and over mountain passes, these carriers of the U.S. Mail rode with their precious cargo, a water bag and a revolver. The greatest ride on record was recorded by a rider named, Jack Keetly, covering some three hundred forty miles in a single journey.

Sadly, although it made for great story telling, it was a business that never made money. Initially the cost of a single ounce of mail was five dollars, a considerable sum at the time. But there were too few customers to pay for all those riders, over four hundred horses and the upkeep of nearly a hundred and eighty relay stations. Just eighteen months after its inception, the business that had started with such great fanfare in April of 1860 made its last run in late October of 1861. In all fairness, it was a business that was doomed to early extinction as the eventual stringing of telegraph lines between Missouri and Nevada would spell the end of the costly labor-intensive enterprise.

Eventually, the mail service would be taken up by the slower but more economical Butterfield Stagecoach line, which was eventually purchased by another American icon, a little company called, Wells-Fargo.

What the brave riders did prove, in those eighteen months that made legends of young men like Jack Keetley, Robert *Pony Bob* Haslam and *Buffalo Bill* Cody, was that a northern route across the plains of Nebraska, Wyoming, Utah and Nevada was feasible, and it would be their efforts that would eventually mark the course that would become the transcontinental railroad.

Its logo lives on today in the form of a rider on a pony, and is officially claimed as the property of The U.S. Postal service, which trademarked the name and logo in 2006.

A lone rider on a horse rushing into the dead of night; the stuff that legend is made of: the legend of a company whose short life will long be remembered as...

The Pony Express.

Polo, Anyone?

Almost everyone has met someone who had an unusual combination of first and last names. A quick *Google* search will turn up all sorts of combinations, most of them purportedly true, although some are suspicious. Names like: Harry Chin, Eileen Dover, Rusty Karr, Rob Banks are just a few of the clean examples. The famed sports announcer Harry Carey comes to mind, and I would be willing to bet that somewhere there is a man named Justin Case. Of course, there are plenty of offerings that harken back to the eighth grade, but I think I'll just let them go without further comment.

One of the most unusual names in history belonged to a woman known as the *First Lady of Texas*. She was the only daughter of the flamboyant Governor of the state, James S. "Big Jim" Hogg who named his daughter, Ima, or Ima Hogg. By the way, there is a popular myth that Governor Hogg also had a daughter named Ura, but that is not true; Governor Hogg only had one daughter and two sons; another urban myth debunked.

Most people will not change their name; there's probably a boy named Sue somewhere, and just out of curiosity, I looked up Adolf Hitler in an online phone book of the United States. I found two.

People change their names for all sorts of reasons. Lloyd B. Free became World Be Free. Cassius Clay became Muhammad Ali when he became a Black Muslim. Marilyn Monroe was born Norma Jean Baker and one of my favorites, Margaret Mary Emily Anne Hyra is better known as, Meg Ryan. And the list goes on.

Today's story is about a family name that was changed because, well, it was embarrassing, and here's how it goes.

In 1939, a baby boy was born in the Bronx borough of New York City to proud parents, Jewish immigrants named Fraydl and Frank Lifshitz. They named their new son, Ralph, one of three brothers, two of whom were troubled by the name which, with a little imagination and a lack of good taste, could be turned into something less than complimentary. By the time young Ralph had turned sixteen, his older brother, Terry, who by that time had become Ralph's legal guardian, decided he'd had enough of the torment that came with the name Lifshitz, and had it changed legally. It seemed like a no-brainer at the time; they'd had some cousins who underwent a name change out in California, changing their last name to, Lawrence; although later in life brother Ralph would have to fend off suggestions that he had changed his name to downplay his Jewish heritage. It was not the case.

In 1957, Ralph graduated from the Dewitt Clinton High School in the Bronx where his stated goal that appeared alongside his yearbook photo, was to "become a millionaire." A lot of people have the dream. Ralph would not be disappointed.

He would embark on a journey that started before high school graduation, where he made a little side money by selling neckties to his fellow classmates. Ralph had a keen eye for fashion and his little necktie business would one day be the beginning of something much bigger indeed. After a couple of years of college, Ralph dropped out of school and joined the Army for a two year stint before taking a job as a salesman at New York's venerable, Brooks Brothers.

Within a year, this future master of fashion design had created his own line of neckties and with the help of a clothing manufacturer named,

Norman Hilton, introduced the ties to the world under the brand name, Polo.

The rest is pretty much history, the Polo line of clothing and its designer would go on to win the prestigious COTY award for his line of menswear in 1970. In 1972, the now classic *Polo* mesh short sleeve shirt was introduced in a full range of twenty-four different colors.

Soon, a line of suits for women tailored in a classic male cut and carrying the *Polo* logo were all the rage and the fashion dynasty of the boy from the Bronx was on its way. Sportswear, formal wear, a line of fragrances, accessories, even a distinctive line of paint colors for the home handyman were all part of the array that fall under the trademark of the company started by a young man with a dream.

It has been a dream come true, that ranks this superstar of couture, number 187 on the Forbes list of the richest people in the world, with a net worth estimated at just under six billion dollars. That will buy a lot of neckties!

Not bad for a designer who started out as Ralph Lifshitz but now goes by the name of...

Ralph Lauren.

Exquisite Timepiece

It is written that, *"on the fourth day, God made two great lights; one to rule the day, and one to rule the night,"* and from that moment on, the Earth has been governed by time; one moment flowing into another from one day to the next.

Today's story is about how we measure those moments of time and about the company whose <u>timepieces</u> are among the most respected in the world.

Unlike the rest of the animal kingdom, humans always want to know what time it is. It's how we schedule things. It's how airlines and railroads and radio programs work. It's how the British know when to serve tea or when we Americans can start the Super Bowl. Our lives are governed by the relentless tic-tock of a timepiece somewhere.

During the day, it's pretty easy to tell time, even without a watch. We simply track the sun as is moves across the sky. Up in the east and down in the west in that great circular arc that we all know so well. The ancients knew that you could track the movement of the sun by tracking its shadow, and that is how the sundial came into existence. It was a lot easier on the eyes than staring at the Sun. As far as anyone can remember nobody ever went blind looking at a sundial.

Sundials were so highly regarded by the Romans that donors of public sundials had their names inscribed on them. Wealthy Romans even had little pocket sundials that they could carry around with them.

Of course, the big problem with sundials is that the sun goes down; every day for most of us. It's a little trickier at the North and South Poles, but let's not worry about that today.

Anyway, somebody had to come up with a way of telling time...at night.

The first idea was the water clock. It marked time by measuring water that filled up in a tank. It had a series of gears that moved a pointer on a dial. The great thing about it was that it worked at night as long as the water didn't freeze.

Then came something called, *the astrolabe*. It worked at night also and it was about as complicated a gizmo as you can get. It's so complicated that by the time you figured out what time it was, the sun came up and you could go back to using the sundial.

Next came the *candle clock*. The Encyclopedia Britannica says the first mention of a candle clock is around 900A.D. But it's probably much older. The candle clock was pretty simple; draw a notch on a candle and mark how long it takes the wick to get there. It worked well at night as long as there wasn't much of a breeze.

Finally, around the tail end of the thirteenth century somebody had the idea to make the first mechanical clock. It used weights and gravity to power a set of gears that moved a dial, and it was the grandmother of the modern timepiece. A lot of grandfather clocks still use the weight and gravity system.

In the early 15th century somebody figured out that a coiled spring could replace the weights of the gravity clock, and the portable time piece was a reality. People who could afford it could carry a timepiece with them, only now it didn't poke a hole in your trousers they way those pocket sundials must have done back in the days of Caesar. For the most part, watches were carried by gentlemen, and carried in a vest pocket.

But, in 1868, that started to change. The first <u>wristwatch</u> was created by two watchmakers by the names of, Antoni Patek and Adrien Phillipe. Their company, *Patek-Phillipe*, is one of the oldest watchmaking companies still in existence. At the time, the wristwatch was considered unmanly. However, by the 1880's the German Navy realized its obvious practicality and commissioned the watchmaking firm of Girard-Perregaux to supply one for all of its officers. By 1903, over ninety thousand wristwatches were selling annually in Germany. Nobody was about to question the manliness of a German naval officer.

Worldwide sales were given a shot in the arm because of an aviation pioneer named, Albert Santos-Dumont, who was the heir to a Brazilian coffee empire. Santos-Dumont found that fumbling around with a pocket watch while he was trying to steer a hot air balloon was a nuisance, so he asked his friend, Louis Cartier, to design a special watch. And from that moment on, the wristwatch became a growth industry as the pocket watch headed down the same road as the horse and buggy.

Soon everybody was making wristwatches including two London merchants by the names of Hans Wilsdorf and Alfred Davis. They weren't true watchmakers, but they were in the business; buying watch <u>movements</u> from Switzerland and then putting them into cases they had made locally. W&D, as it was known at the time, was the creator of what is probably the best known of all the designer watches in the world, and it is where this story is headed.

It is a name that is synonymous with wealth and success. It was the first wristwatch to be certified as a chronometer for its accuracy. The first watch to display the day and the date. One of its watches was submerged to the depths of the Mariana Trench where it operated flawlessly at some 33,000 feet below sea level, the lowest point on Earth. It was worn on Sir Edmund Hilary's history-making ascent of Mt. Everest in 1953.

But,since you, and probably nobody else, has ever heard of a Wilsdorf and Davis, or W&D watch, here's how the W&D came to be called by the name by which the company is better known.

In 1908, Hans Wilsdorf trademarked the now familiar name based, some say, on letters that he picked from the french term *Horlogerie Exquisite* which means, 'exquisite timepiece'. The story was never confirmed by Wilsdorf, but the brand endures today as a symbol of the highest standard in the world of watchmaking.

And the letters that he picked for his *exquisite timepiece...*

R-O-L-E and X...what we know as...

Rolex

Another Watch Story

In 1886, a Chicago jewelery manufacturer sent an unsolicited shipment of gold-filled watches to a jeweler in North Redwood, Minnesota. The Minnesota jeweler had no use for the product and refused to take delivery; and that accidental shipment would serve as the seed of one of the most successful retail companies in the world. But first, a bit of history.

Most people understand, correctly, that the completion of the transcontinental railroad in 1869 created a continuous link between the east and west coasts of the United States, but it did a great deal more than that. It opened up the vast great plains and the arid west to new settlement. Tragically, in doing so it also brought an end to the culture and tradition of the many tribes of Native Americans who had been the virtual sole occupants of the land for thousands of years. Such is the way of the world.

But with each trainload of new inhabitants came farms and towns and businesses that still exist today, and all of the inhabitants of those new towns needed tools, machinery, seed, dry goods and every imaginable commodity with which to build an ever expanding America. And since there were few stores and warehouses to supply them, they relied on *mail-order*. Interestingly, mail order in the U.S. was begun by Benjamin Franklin, who made money as far back as 1744 selling books through the mails. Franklin even offered a money-back guarantee.

The first large scale mail-order business was started in New York City in 1848 by Alfred Hammacher. If that name rings a bell, it's the same Hammacher of the giant Hammacher-Schlemmer company whose catalogs are found in the reading pouches of just about every commercial airline in the country. But that's not the end of the story.

The most successful of the early mail-order catalog houses in the country was started in 1872 by a man named, Arron Montgomery Ward. Montgomery Ward sold almost anything you could imagine and helped supply America with everything under the sun. You could even buy a complete build-it-yourself house kit through the Ward's catalog. Unfortunately, Ward's retail operation went out of business in 2001, although the catalog business is still alive.

But that's still not the end of the story, because it was in 1886, fourteen years after Ward had started his mail order company, that an unimaginable rival was founded that would eventually help put an end to the once dominant Montgomery Ward chain and become one of the largest retail companies in the world; which brings us back to that shipment of gold watches that nobody wanted. Because, as it turns out, one young man did want them.

He was a young railway agent who stepped up to the plate and bought the entire shipment of watches that the Minnesota jeweler had rejected. The agent was an employee of the Minneapolis and St. Louis Railway, who worked at the company's North Redwood location. Just twenty-seven years old, we'll call him, Richard Warren. Richard was a young man, whose salary left something to be desired, so, to make ends meet, he had supplemented his income from time to time by selling coal and lumber to nearby farmers. When the shipment of watches became available, he did what every entrepreneur does...he took a chance. He bought the entire shipment figuring that he could sell them to other station agents and contacts along the railway line. He guessed right, and within a few months had tucked away a tidy profit. Enough of a profit that he bought more watches, and within the year, Richard had founded a watch company in Minneapolis that bears his name today. Now, while Richard knew how to <u>sell</u> watches, he didn't know how to repair them, so a year later, now living in Chicago, he placed an ad in the Chicago Daily News that read as follows:

Wanted: *Watchmaker with reference who can furnish tools. State age, experience and salary required.*

The young man who answered that ad would make make one of the smartest business decisions in history. He was a twenty-two year old watch maker from Lafayette, Indiana whom we'll call Alvah Curtis for now.

Richard and Alvah soon became friends would go into partnership and form a company in 1893 with both of their names on the masthead. By 1895, the company was boasting some $750,000 in annual sales and on its way to becoming the powerhouse that it is today. But then, something changed. Richard was looking for some fresh money to give the company a financial boost, and brought in an outsider, a clothing manufacturer named, Julius Rosenwald, who bought into the company and reorganized it.

By most accounts, Rosenwald was something of an organizational genius, who used his skills to streamline the company which was badly in need of some efficiency. There's a story on the company website that one customer who had received <u>ten</u> sewing machines by mistake sent a letter pleading with the company not to send any more. Julius Rosenwald straightened all of that out, and within a few months, the company's shipping process was so efficient that, years later, automaker Henry Ford visited the operation to see what he could learn from it. Rosenwald was so good that Richard promoted him to the number two slot in the firm, ahead of co-founder Alvah. It was a move that forever changed the company, but not its name.

Already suffering from ill-health, Alvah asked Richard to buy him out for the modest sum of $20,000, that he would eventually invest in a company that made motion picture projectors. It ranks as one of the biggest mistakes in the history of business decisions. Alvah had unknowingly left a fortune on the table, although he never complained about it, and eventually would rejoin his old firm to write its corporate history.

And the rest is history. This retail giant, born from a mail-order watch company, would go on to create the *Allstate Insurance Company* and the *Discover Card*, and own what for a time was the tallest building in the world. It's now part of a conglomerate that also owns *K-Mart* with annual sales in excess of fifty billion dollars.

A company started by two young men, Richard Warren **Sears**, and Alvah Curtis **Roebuck** founders of...*Sears Roebuck and Company*.

The Whale and the Coffee Bean

One of the best known lines in all of English literature is, "call me Ishmael," which of course the opening line of Herman Melville's classic novel of obsession, revenge, good and evil, and of course a great white whale by the name of, *Moby Dick*. There is a great old movie of the story with Gregory Peck as Captain Ahab, Richard Basehart as Ishmael and a host of others who played the crew of the whaling ship, The Pequod, as it sailed the North Atlantic. And, if you are a good trivia buff, you will figure out the connection between Moby Dick and the story of ...coffee.

Here in the United States we think of coffee as somehow "ours." After all, coffee became the national drink fairly soon after a group calling itself, *The Sons of Liberty,* dressed up as Narragansett Indians and threw a couple of tons of tea into Boston Harbor in what has become known as the Boston Tea Party, but there's a lot more to it than that.

Most historians agree that the Tea Party was the beginning of our national preference for coffee, but the commercial appeal of coffee was undoubtedly bolstered by the slave trade and its connection to the coffee fields of Brazil. Whatever the reason, America is a nation of coffee-lovers, a drink that traces its origins back to Africa and more specifically to Ethiopia where legend has it that the eye-popping stay-awake effects of the coffee bean were first discovered by a goat herder by the name of Kaldi sometime around the ninth century. And, in fact if you do a *Google* search of Kaldi, you'll find all sorts of coffee shops and even a major distributor with the name Kaldi or some variation of the name.

It is most likely that the Kaldi story is a myth but in any case, coffee as a drink didn't get into full swing until five or six hundred years later, when it made its way north to the Arab world, where it caught on like crazy. But there's definitely an Ethiopian connection. The English word *coffee*, comes from the Dutch, *Koffe*, which comes from the Turkish *Khava* which comes from the Ethiopian Kingdom of *Kaffe*.

Anyway, it was the Arabs who first had the idea to roast the coffee 'cherries' as they're called, grind them into powder and then brew them in hot water, pretty much the way we do today. Then, for the most part, it was the Dutch, who brought coffee to Europe. The Dutch were always good at finding new goodies to trade around the world. I mention this because the Dutch got their coffee from a port in Yemen by the name of...*Mocha,* another word associated with coffee. In fact, the Dutch influence circles the globe, as it was they who introduced coffee to Indonesia, where it was first planted on the island of *Java,* still another word for coffee.

Here's a curious bit of history. As most people know, ever since the Crusades there has been a certain amount of, let's say, "tension" between Christians and Muslims, to put it mildly. And, since coffee came from the heart of the Muslim world, it was generally viewed with suspicion by westerners. That is, until Pope Clement VIII had a taste of it. Clement had been urged by his advisers to ban the drink as being the, "bitter invention of Satan." But the story goes that, after his first cup, Pope Clement decided it was so delicious that it ought to be baptized instead of banned, and since the Christian world was pretty much Catholic at the time, coffee got the religious equivalent of the Good Housekeeping Seal of Approval, and it has been with us ever since.

That was around the year 1600, and soon after, coffee got the green light. Coffee <u>houses</u> started opening up everywhere. For the record, in both England and France, women were banned from coffee houses except as wait staff, meaning that the places were mostly populated with men who had nothing better to do than sit around drinking coffee, smoking tobacco and reading the paper all day. (and people say that television ruined the world)

That's pretty much the story of the coffee house, so let's fast-forward a few centuries to the coffee house in America.

Up until about 1980, the American coffee house was a kind of 'beat' hangout in college towns, where really hip people would sit around smoking Balkan Sobranie cigarettes and reciting poetry from real hip guys like Alan Ginsberg and Lawrence Ferlinghetti. Those beatniks sure knew how to party.

But, in the 1980s, the coffeehouse went mainstream. It went from selling plain old coffee to selling the super-potent Italian version called, *espresso*, which is finely ground coffee that is brewed by forcing steam and hot water through a strainer. By the way, it's pronounced, ES-*presso* not Ex-*presso*. The 'X' comes from the Spanish spelling. Now you know.

In 1981, a plastics salesman by the name of, Howard Shultz, called on three guys named Jerry Baldwin, Zev Siegl, and Gordon Bowker. The trio had started a business in 1971 selling, not coffee drinks, but specialty coffee <u>beans</u> to customers in Seattle. The company got on Shultz's radar screen because it had been selling a lot of plastic thermos bottles to its customers, and Schultz happened to rep the company that made the plastic bottles. After a couple of twists and turns, Howard became the marketing director of the coffee bean company and one day he had a bright idea; turn the coffee <u>bean</u> business into a coffee <u>bar</u> business. The owners hated the idea. The last thing they wanted to do was run a restaurant.

But Howard Shultz wasn't the kind of guy who took 'no' for an answer. He persuaded owner, Jerry Baldwin to let him open a little coffee bar in the corner of the coffee bean store...and it caught on like hotcakes. Four years later, in 1987, Howard Shultz and a group of investors bought out the remaining owners for, get this, 3.7 million dollars, which today seems like peanuts. (or beans)

So, what does any of this have to do with Captain Ahab chasing the great white whale, *Moby Dick*, all over the North Atlantic?

The name of that little coffee bean company in Seattle was taken from the Herman Melville novel, which takes place on the whaling ship, *The Pequod*, whose first mate was a sailor who called himself...

Starbucks.

Tickling The Ivories

If you've ever bought anything very expensive, someone always says, "you're paying for the name." Of course, there's a reason that you pay for the name and today's story is about one of those names.

There's an old joke about musicians that I still love. Question: how do you get a rock guitarist to turn down his amplifier? The answer is: put sheet music in front of him. Nowadays, very few people read sheet music.

But the sheet music business used to be big, That was before Thomas Edison invented the phonograph. Up until then, if you wanted music in the home. You had to make it...or rather <u>play</u> it yourself, and a lot of people did. People would hear a piece of music at a concert or a bar or in church and they'd would go down to the sheet music store and pick up a couple of tunes, much the way we play *iTunes* today.

Anyway, sheet music needs to be played on something and in the nineteenth century the instrument of choice was, the piano. Because, pianos can do it all...play the accompaniment and the lead. You don't get that with a violin or a trumpet. The piano; that uniquely beautiful wooden sculpture, with the eighty-eight keys that used to be made of ebony for the black keys and ivory for the whites. It's pretty hard to find ivory keys anymore, because there is an international ban on harvesting the stuff from living animals, after poachers had just about wiped out the elephant; and frankly, it does seem pretty immoral to wipe out an entire species just so Hoagy Carmichael can play "Stardust" in a saloon.

In case you're wondering, all tolled, there are about 12,000 parts in a piano which means that pianos are essentially hand-made.

It has been my observation that most people who own pianos can barely play them. For the most part, the piano is just a piece of furniture waiting patiently for someone to caress it and make it come to life. Playing the piano has become something of a lost art now that the guitar has taken control of pop music, and <u>real</u> pianos have been replaced by digital keyboards, which can sound a lot like pianos if you get a good one. One thing for sure; a digital piano is a heck of a lot easier to move, since it doesn't weigh a thousand pounds.

By the way, *Piano* is an Italian word meaning *soft*. Pianos were originally called *pianofortes*, *forte* meaning strong or in the case of music...*loud*. There used to be something called a... *forte piano*. It's actually where the piano got its start. It was invented by an Italian by the name of Bartolomeo Christofori around 1700. It sounded a lot like a harpsichord, only worse. I'm not a big fan of harpsichords.

The modern piano has come along way. For one thing, it's gotten bigger over the years. Eighty-eight keys are now the standard, which makes them so big that they have to have a large iron plate to keep the whole thing from buckling under the pressure created by the pull of the strings; there's about eighteen <u>tons</u> of *pull* on an upright and maybe thirty tons on a concert grand. The iron plate idea was patented by a guy named, Alpheus Babcock, who later went to work for a company called *Chickering*, and they still make a good piano.

Here's a fun bit of history, well my idea of fun. The upper 'A' note on a piano is tuned to 440 cycles per second. That's the standard "concert pitch". I only bring it up because the standard is somewhat arbitrary. It was actually set by the Nazi propaganda minister, Joseph Goebbels. The Nazi's couldn't get up in the morning without figuring how to interfere with somebody else's business. Before the Nazi's, pianos were tuned to whatever the concert master liked. Giuseppe Verdi...you know the guy who wrote *La Traviata* and *Rigoletto*...was convinced that "A-440" as it is called, ruined the voices of opera singers and wanted pianos tuned down a couple of notches to 432 cycles per second. Anyway...the sound we take for granted has only been standard for seventy years.

There are a lot of pretty good pianos, Jazz players really like *Yamaha's,* and they make an excellent piano. *Baldwin* has been making outstanding pianos since the 1850's. There's a company called, *Bosendorfer,* that you see on the concert stage. But, for the vast majority of concert level players, there is one name that stands out from all the others.

So here is, as someone once said, the rest of the story. In 1850, Henry Englehard Steinway brought his family to New York from Germany where he had built over four hundred pianos. In 1853, he opened a shop in Manhattan with a dream and a vision, to build *"the best piano possible; to always build to a standard...never to a price"*

Steinway basically reinvented the grand piano. Grands used to be rectangular; what we now call a "square grand." All the strings ran horizontally at right angles to the keys. Nobody does that anymore. It's really no way to make a piano, because doing it that way meant that each key had a slightly different "feel". Not a good Idea.

Steinway had a better idea which he borrowed from a guy named Jean-Henri Pape. It's called the *overstrung layout.* It basically runs strings diagonally across the piano to give them more length, which creates a much richer sound, especially in the bass notes. Clever idea. Everybody who played the piano thought so too, and by the late 1800's, Steinway was turning out 3,500 pianos a year. Steinway also created the modern piano case, with the familiar curved side in the treble section...(those are the high notes for those of you who weren't paying attention in music class.) It takes a lot of effort to bend the wood, and Steinway patented that process as well.

So what makes a Steinway so special? A couple of thoughts. Remember how a piano is really a *Piano Forte*...soft and loud? It's pretty easy to make a loud piano. The hard part is making one that can be played softly. By re-arranging the strings, Steinway made all the keys <u>feel</u> the same and once you do that, and add in about 130 other patented innovations, you've created a piano that has a rather amazing depth of sound; a piano that can be played both loudly <u>and</u> softly.

 The other part is quality and consistency: it takes about a year to make a Steinway Grand...nothing is ever rushed. This is important because concert pianists like to play on something that feels like the piano they have at home, and unlike a violin...you can't just pop a piano into the overhead storage bin on a 747. So, it's important that when you play the "house piano" at Carnegie Hall it should feel familiar, like an old friend...and, for the most part, a Steinway in New York will play and feel just like a Steinway in Chicago or London or Buenos Aires, which is why every great concert pianist from Paderewski to Van Cliburn to Harry Connick, Jr. has played on a Steinway.

By the way, if you are interested in buying one of the things, take a deep breath. A new Steinway "Baby Grand " or "S" model (they come in S, M and L...just like shirts) will set you back about fifty grand. If you're tight for cash, I saw a two year old *S* model on Ebay for $46,000. The bigger pianos cost more.

One last cool tidbit...Steinway trades on the New York Stock Exchange under the ticker symbol, *LVB*...the initials of a composer you may have heard of; a fellow German named, Ludwig **van B**eethoven.

And that's the story of a family business that created, "The Instrument of the Immortals"...

Steinway and Sons

A Little Drop of Fire

If the name, Jean Hector Crevecoeur, means nothing to you, you're not alone. Most people have never heard of him. He was a friend of Benjamin Franklin and Ethan Allen among others. A Frenchman and naturalized citizen of the United States, Crevecoeur is most famous for something that he wrote in the late 1700's; a series of essays entitled, *Letters from An American Farmer,* in which he described an America where, "individuals of all nations are *melted* into a new race of men, whose labors and posterity will one day cause great changes in the world." And, although he never used the exact phrase, it is from his work that the term "melting pot" originated; the words that are often used to described the uniquely American mix of people and culture.

Most Americans tend to think of themselves as members of a single nation. We probably got that way from reciting the Pledge of Allegiance in grade school, with its ever-present reminder that we are, indeed, "one nation under God." However, when the country was first organized, we thought very differently. We were a group of separate countries, or States if you will, each with its own identity, heroes and history. But the one thing that the original thirteen colonies had in common was that they were unequivocally, British. After all, it was from Great Britain that we won our independence. Not from France or

Spain, even though both of those countries held vast tracks of land in North America. The men we call the founding fathers were all subjects of the British Empire; George Washington, Thomas Jefferson, Ben Franklin all the way down to John Hancock.

One undeniable fact of the American Revolution is that we were able to gain our independence from England, in part, with help from the French who didn't much like the English back in those days. It's a rivalry that has been going on for about a thousand years. It hasn't done either of them much good, but it has worked out pretty well for us.

In the Revolutionary War, The French sent arms and men to help us fight the English. We might have won without their help, but you never know with this sort of thing. If it hadn't been for the French, we might still be closing our saloons in the afternoon to have a spot of tea.

Anyway, after our Revolutionary War, the French and the English were still at it, and in 1803, the French, under the leadership of Napoleon, needed money to try and finish the English off once and for all. So, Napoleon approached President Thomas Jefferson with a deal; to sell all of the land around the Mississippi river to us for the grand sum of fifteen million dollars. Now, in those days fifteen million was some real money. Today, it might not even get you a minor league baseball team. Tells you a little bit about what the politicians have done to the U.S. Dollar, doesn't it? Anyway, Jefferson took the deal which we now call, the *Louisiana Purchase* and it worked out pretty well for us.

We ended up with 828,000 square miles of new land, and all or part of what would eventually become fourteen new states including the territory known as, Louisiana, with its rich fabric of French, Spanish, Caribbean, African and native-American culture; its language, legal system, and best of all...its cuisine. Louisiana was and remains the essence of the melting pot that was described by Crevecoeur.

And, all of a sudden, great new exotic-sounding delicacies were part of the now-broadened potpourri of the American diet. Things like jambalaya, gumbo and Etouffee were no longer the exclusive fare of foreigners and riverboat gamblers. The bland food of the British diet now had a competitor in the aromatic, and spicy offerings of New Orleans and the Mississippi delta.

Now, if there's one thing that separates southern food from that of say, New England, it's hot sauce. I spent a lot of time in New England in my youth, and when I was a kid, if you asked for hot sauce, they thought you meant mustard.

But, down South, hot sauce is a world of its own, an entire cosmos of peppery concoctions with colorful names like *Blair's Death Rain, Texas Pete's, Dave's Liquid Insanity* and a host of others. But the grandaddy of them all was the creation of a man by the name of, Edmund McIlhenny, who developed his unique product in the late 1860's.

According to the family history, McIlhenny, an avid gardener and food lover, was given a supply of imported seeds from Mexico that are part of the Cayenne pepper family. He planted them on Avery Island, a giant salt dome that lies roughly a hundred and forty miles west of New Orleans. McIlhenny harvested the peppers, selecting only "the very reddest of the red," which he then crushed and added to a blend of french red wine vinegar and Avery Island salt. He let the entire "mash", as he called it, sit for at least thirty days in barrels and crockery jars.

When that peppery sauce was finally decanted from its original mash, it was hot. So hot that McIlhenny poured it into little perfume or cologne bottles so that it would only pour a single drop at a time.

It was referred to as, "the sauce that Mr. McIlhenny makes" and was so popular among family and friends that, in 1868, he harvested his first commercial crop and sold six hundred and fifty-eight bottles to local grocers in and around New Orleans. Suffice it to say that the product was a huge success. So much so that, in 1870, he received a patent for it. All it needed now was a name.

The name that he gave it, which is still used today, was a word that Edmund McIlhenny believed to be of Mexican and Indian origin and meant, "place where the soil is humid."

And today, according to the company website, the sauce is still made much the same way as it was originally. It is a product that is labeled in twenty-two languages and dialects, sold in over 160 countries and territories, and put on restaurant tables around the globe. It is the most famous, most preferred pepper sauce in the world. That zesty little creation in the familiar little bottle that dribbles one fiery drop at a time because it was meant to be, "sprinkled, not poured."

That little drop of fire that Edmund McIlhenny called...

Tabasco.

The Empty Cylinder

Every December 7th, Americans mark the anniversary of the attack on Pearl Harbor; the attack that drew the United States into the second World War and ended just a few days after we dropped the atomic bomb, first on Hiroshima and then on Nagasaki, in 1945. Today's story is about the rather bizarre set of circumstances that aided the development of the atomic bomb and one of the amazing spinoffs from the bomb that can be found in the kitchen, the bathroom, your car, and is probably in your carpet.

The irony of the story is that before we can get to the atomic bomb, which produces heat in the tens of millions of degrees, we have to start at the other end of the physics scale, namely, refrigeration.

Prior to about 1915, if you wanted to keep something cold, you put it in the "ice box"; literally a big cabinet filled with ice. The ice usually came from caverns under lakes where it had been stored over the winter.

As a practical matter, refrigeration came into existence in the 1850's with the invention of the first ice-making machine. Home refrigerators came along about fifty years later. I'm not going to go into what makes a refrigerator work, but the basic idea starts with a gas that stays cold under pressure.

Now, for about fifty years, commercial refrigerators used gases like ammonia and sulfur dioxide. They kept the food cool, but if they ever leaked, you basically ended up with a toxic gas spill inside your kitchen. Not a great idea, especially if you're having guests over to the house for dinner.

So, the people at General Motors decided to do something about it. GM got involved because, aside from making Chevrolets and Cadillacs, GM was also made a refrigerator, which they called the *FrigidAire*. Well aware of the dangers of the existing refrigeration technology, GM wanted something that wouldn't kill you if it sprung a leak. Not a bad idea. So they turned to one of their chemists, a guy named Thomas Midgley, who experimented with chlorine and fluorine and eventually ended up with a compound called *Freon* that was later manufactured by DuPont. Most people are familiar with Freon. It's what we used in refrigerators and air conditioners until we decided that it was killing the earth's ozone layer. Freon was keeping our soda pop cool, but, unfortunately, we were getting fried by the sun in the process. Not really a great tradeoff, which is why we now use something else.

Anyway, in 1938 a chemist at DuPont by the name of Roy Plunkett, was working to find something that would make refrigerators more efficient, and one of his experiments became known as *the case of the empty cylinder*. It was an experiment that led to something truly amazing. Plunkett mixed up a batch of what he hoped would be a new and improved version of freon. He put the mixture into one of those big metal cylinders that hold gas under pressure, and went home for the evening.

When he arrived at work the next morning, he made a startling discovery; there was no gas in the cylinder, or so it seemed. Naturally, he checked for leaks, but there weren't any. Very surprising, indeed. Then he weighed the empty cylinder, only to discover that it wasn't empty at all. There was something in there, but Plunkett had to cut the thing open to find out what it was. And what he found was a waxy white powder that nobody had ever seen before. The gas in the cylinder had formed a completely new compound; something called, *Poly-Tetra-Fluro-Ethylene,* or <u>PTFE</u> for short. Don't worry, DuPont came up with a better name.

What made PTFE amazing was that is was...good for nothing! Lab workers poured acids and bases on it, and it would just sit there. Nothing affected it. It wouldn't dissolve <u>into</u> anything either. You could heat it up and it wouldn't melt, and anything you poured onto it just ran off the stuff the way water beads off a freshly-waxed car. It was virtually inert; meaning it wouldn't interact with anything, physically or chemically. And, being inert, there really wasn't much use for the stuff. It was nothing more than a lot of useless goo headed for the scrap heap.

Then, purely by chance, in 1942, an Army General by the name of Leslie Groves heard about the stuff and had a brilliant idea. Groves was the guy who had overseen the building of the Pentagon, and he did such a great job on that project that he was given a new assignment. It was called the *Manhattan Project,* which as most of you know was the program that ultimately led to the creation of the atomic bomb.

General Groves had a problem; to make the atom bomb you need enriched uranium, and to do that, engineers had to work with a nasty chemical called *Uranium Hexafluoride* or what they call *HEX.* No HEX...no bomb. But the problem with HEX is that it <u>eats</u> everything; pipes, gaskets, liners...you name it and Uranium Hexafluoride will eat it. And, if they couldn't solve that problem, the Manhattan Project would end up a dud. That's when General Groves asked a question:

Would the super-corrosive Uranium Hexafluoride also eat that waxy-good-for-nothing-slippery-as-all-get-out goo that Roy Plunkett had discovered in 1938? The answer was a resounding, NO! It was just what Groves was looking for.

So, DuPont mixed up a boatload of PTFE to coat the pipes and gaskets used at the Oak Ridge plant in Tennessee, enabling scientists to harvest enough enriched uranium to make the atomic bomb.

The only trouble they had with the whole process is that since PTFE doesn't stick to anything, the whiz kids at Du Pont had to come up with a special etching process just to get it to coat the surfaces of whatever they wanted it to stick to. (I am hoping my sixth grade teacher will forgive ending a sentence with a preposition, but it is my story)

What Roy Plunkett had really discovered was something that DuPont would later trademark under its now familiar name. It was so special that DuPont couldn't even produce it commercially until the end of World War II, when it was officially declassified as a military secret.

That slippery PTFE has come a long way, and now it's everywhere. Silicon valley uses it to make computer chips. It's injected into your wiper blades to keep them from squeaking. *Gore-Tex* uses the stuff to keep you from sweating, even in the rain. DuPont uses it in its *Stainmaster* carpet to, well, keep the stains out. It's even used in the Statue of Liberty as a lubricant so that the copper skin of Lady Liberty won't rub on the steel frame that holds her up. But most of us remember its first commercial application, which came after the war, when Du Pont had the idea to put it onto <u>frying pans</u> to keep your scrambled eggs from sticking.

It is a truly amazing product that we all use every day, that was discovered almost entirely by chance.

And that's how the search for safer refrigeration found its way into the Manhattan Project and jumped out of the atomic fire and into the frying pan as something we call.....*Teflon.*

A Place to Call Home

One of the things that make a good conversation interesting is the fact that it has no agenda. You don't know where you're going to end up once you get started. It's so totally different from, say, a business meeting, where there's a clear agenda and you are dragged along with it, whether you like it or not.

I mention this because, the other day I was having lunch with an old friend in one of Denver's fashionable Cherry Creek restaurants, and as is my custom, happened to order a bourbon Old-fashioned to get things started. The cocktail was acceptable, but just, and I commented to my friend that you would think that with a name like *Old-fashioned*, every bartender would know how to make one, being so old-fashioned and all. Not so. The two of us agreed that, if you want to get a really good drink, served they way they did it in the old days, you have to go to a really good hotel.

This led to a conversation about all the hotels where we had enjoyed the privilege of dining, drinking or rooming over the years. For the record, my home town of Denver has a first class hotel in the Brown Palace which has been a favorite of mine since I first was introduced to it as a teenager. No, I wasn't drinking. Well, not Old-fashioneds anyway.

We talked about hotels like The Drake in Chicago, The Mark Hopkins and the Fairmont in San Francisco, The Grosvenor House and the Savoy in London, and my personal favorite, The George V in Paris, to name just a few. I have left out, probably the most famous hotel in the world because that is the subject of today's story, but before we get there, we have to talk a little about the fur trade and "the richest man in America.".

Our story begins with a sixteen year-old German who began his career working as an assistant to his father, a traveling butcher who lived in west central Germany, near Heidelberg. The young man was named, John Jacob Astor. In 1779, the young Astor emigrated to London and shortly thereafter moved to the newly formed United States. While making the voyage to Baltimore, Astor made friends with a fur trader, who convinced the young man that a fortune could be made selling furs to Europeans.

It was as good a time to be in the business as anyone could ever imagine. Newly signed treaties between the now liberated colonies and Great Britain fostered tremendous trade between the two nations. America was virtually abundant in its supply of fur, and there was seemingly no end to Europe's demand.

Astor took a job at an established fur trading house in Baltimore and soon proved that he had a keen mind for business. Within a very short number of years, Astor had managed to establish his own business and became the exclusive supplier of furs to some of the most fashionable furriers in London. Within a few years, the entrepreneurial Astor had virtually cornered the North American fur trade. It was the beginning of one of the greatest personal fortunes in American history, but only the beginning. For John Jacob Astor would soon discover, here in America, something that was only a pipe dream for most Europeans; the investment magic of...Real Estate.

Over several years, Astor parlayed the earnings from the fur business into vast real estate holdings, mostly in Manhattan and the other boroughs of New York, eventually owning more than seven hundred income-producing properties. One of his better known deals was one that he made with then vice-President Aaron Burr, for a piece of land near Central Park, that Astor promptly subdivided into two hundred and fifty lots, which he sold off to eager investors.

At the time of his death in 1848, Astor was said to be worth somewhere between thirty and fifty million dollars...an amount which in 2010 dollars would have been well over a billion dollars, making this butcher's son one of the wealthiest men in U.S. History, and certainly the richest man in America at the time.[1]

But the story doesn't stop there. All of that money eventually flowed to sons and grandsons alike, most of whom managed to increase the family fortune. It's amazing how much wealth you could accumulate in this country before there was an income tax.

In 1893, a grandson named William W. Astor decided to build a hotel. I'd tell you what the W stands for, but I'd be giving away the ending. I will tell you that it stands for the town that John Jacob came from originally.

Will built his hotel on 5th Avenue and 34th streets, on the site of his father's mansion, a fact that caused a feud in the family since it was next to the home of his Aunt Caroline. This didn't sit too well with Aunt Caroline, but she was eventually persuaded to move uptown by her son, Will's cousin John Jacob Astor IV, who built a hotel of his own next to William's. The Astors had managed to build two grand hotels in the middle of New York's fifth Avenue. Within a few years, the separate hotels would be connected architecturally, and would stand as a prominent reminder of the family's wealth for nearly a half a century.

Then, in 1931, the entire complex was torn down to make room for a little construction project called, The Empire State building. But that's not quite the end of the story. Because, while the world's then tallest building was being erected, a new hotel was being built on Park Avenue that to this day bears the name of the original; although it is now owned by the Hilton Hotel Corporation, which is a pretty good story of its own.

It has been the home to many notables from time to time, including: the Duke and Duchess of Windsor, Former President Herbert Hoover, General Douglas MacArthur, Marilyn Monroe, Cole Porter and gangster Charles "Lucky" Luciano. It even has its own train station that President Franklin Roosevelt used when he visited New York. If you're rich and you gotta have a crib in the Big Apple, it's is a pretty good place to rest them weary bones after a long day at the office.

And that's the story of a young entrepreneur, named John Jacob Astor, who emigrated to America from a little town in Germany named Waldorf, who made so much money in the fur trade and real estate that his sons and grandsons could build a monument that bears their names even today. A great place to spend an evening, and a great place to find a well-made...Old Fashioned. A place called....

The Waldorf-Astoria.

footnote:

1: Robert Sahr, University of Oregon, Consumer Price Index Conversion Table, 2010; some calculations are much higher, but this is the source I used.

Where's The Beef?

Two things that never cease to amaze me in business are, the inter-connectedness of different businesses, and the amount of room there is for new competitors in existing businesses. Very often, the fortunes of one industry will lead to new developments, both positive and negative, in another industry, although at first blush the two may seem totally unrelated.

An obvious example is the automobile and its relationship to gasoline. Prior to the automobile and its internal combustion engine, gasoline was a novelty by-product of an oil business that was basically only interested in making kerosene for lanterns. With the invention of the carburetor, internal combustion became practicable, and kerosene soon became something of a footnote of history (although it's still used in jet fuel) and car companies started cropping up about as fast as oil derricks in east Texas.

With that in mind, and staying on the subject of cars; when I was a kid, almost every car had two choices of upholstery. You could either get cloth or plastic, or sometimes you could get cloth covered in plastic, so I guess you kind of had three choices. Nobody we ever knew ever had leather seats. Leather seats were for Rolls Royce owners and maybe an occasional Bentley owner. We certainly didn't know any of them. The richest guy on our block was a plumber, and he had an Oldsmobile.

Nowadays, leather has become a commonplace upholstery item; universally included in every luxury car and the preferred seating choice in everything from minivans to SUV's. Even in furniture stores, the cost of leather furniture has come down dramatically over the past twenty years. And what was once reserved for posh sanctuaries like New York's Harvard Club or the sitting rooms of the world's fine hotels, can now be found in living rooms and family rooms in any subdivision in the U.S..

So, why all of a sudden is everybody planting their behind on leather? The answer, plain and simple is: McDonald's. That little California drive-in that made the McDonald brothers and a guy named Ray Kroc rich and famous, has created the demand for enough beef for hamburgers and cheeseburgers to stretch from here to the moon and back. Now, for all that beef, you need a lot of cattle, and from all that cattle comes a heck of a lot of leather.

But this isn't a story about McDonald's. Although the Micky D story is a darn good one.

This is a story about a little girl named Melinda Lou and one of the "me too" companies that came along long after those Golden Arches started popping up like so many blades of grass in a newly sown lawn.

But first, let's get to the cause of all the excitement; The Hamburger.

What most people know is that the hamburger comes from Hamburg, Germany, where it was a ground steak served without a bun. Germany has been the home to a lot of American favorites. The hot dog is sometimes called a frank, short for frankfurter which comes from Frankfurt in Germany. If you'd like to know a really fun bit of history, the Germans are also fond of a pastry that they call, the *Berliner*. And, if you'll remember President Kennedy's famous, *"Ich bin ein Berliner"* speech, although he didn't know it, he was really saying, "I am a jelly doughnut." Most of the crowd seemed to know what he was getting at though, and thought it was a pretty good speech anyway.

What most people don't know is that the hamburger got its origin from the mongols, notably Genghis Khan who liked to eat raw chopped meat after a hard day on the battlefield. When Genghis Khan's grandson, Khublai Khan invaded Russia, he brought the family recipe with him. The Russians didn't much care for the Mongols, but they really liked that Mongolian chopped raw steak, which they called "steak Tartar" since *Tartar* is the Russian word for Mongol.

Okay, so what's the deal with Hamburg? Hamburg is a port city, one of the largest in Europe, and if you know much about world history, you know that sailors are responsible for spreading all sorts of things including language and food, to name just a few.

In the 1600's, sailors from Hamburg sailed to Russia, and when they came back, a lot of *Steak Tartar* came back with them and everybody loved it. It turned out that, if you threw in a lot of onions and spices, you could make the stuff out of fairly inexpensive cuts of beef, so you didn't have to be all that well off to enjoy it. Thus, was born the Hamburger steak, which eventually made its way to New York as more and more Germans emigrated to the U.S. As early as 1834, New York's famed Delmonico's restaurant listed Hamburger Steak on the menu.

Now, Americans love to make things their own, and that's what we did with the hamburger; we put a bun on it, somebody added a slice of cheese, American cheese naturally, and the rest is pretty much history, well almost.

Everybody loves burgers, well except for cows and PETA. PETA is on the record as being anti-burger. I have inferred that cows don't much care for them either.

And just about everybody in America loves cars. It seemed only natural that the two would go hand in hand. I guess if you eat a burger in a car that has leather seats, you've pretty much come full-circle. The evolution of the car and the burger joint seem to run side-by-side like inseparable halves of a two-lane highway stretching from the Atlantic to the Pacific.

Since the 1920's, there have been about a million different hamburger restaurants. Some pretty well known. McDonald's, of course, Burger King, White Castle, Red Robin, Round the Corner, What-a-burger ; The Scotchman Drive-in was a Denver icon in the 50's and 60's. A&W was famous for root beer, but they used it to wash down their burgers.

The list goes on forever, but today's story will end with a guy who started his business in Columbus, Ohio in 1969. A guy whose commercials, in 1984, would ask the question, "Where's the Beef"? His name was Dave Thomas.

Thomas got his start in the food business at a place called, *The Hobby House,* in Ft. Wayne Indiana, where he started as a cook and would eventually own a piece of the business. Along the way, he became friends with the legendary Colonel Harlan Sanders of Kentucky Fried Chicken fame. It's even reported that Dave is the guy who suggested the classic red-striped bucket that is the hallmark of KFC to this day. From Sanders, Dave would learn valuable insights into the business of franchising.

After many years of "paying his dues" and learning the ins and outs of the business, it finally came time for Dave Thomas to open his own restaurant. Looking for a theme, he harkened back to the good old days of one of the hamburger restaurants from his youth. One that he remembered fondly was a place in Kalamazoo, Michigan called, Kewpie Burgers; a company that featured a unique square shaped patty that it served along with an extra-thick milk shake as part of the bill of fare.

On November 15, 1969, Dave Thomas opened his first restaurant; the first of over six thousand five hundred restaurants that are all named after Dave Thomas's then eight-year-old daughter; a little girl named, *Melinda Lou.* If you're wondering why the company isn't called

"Melinda Lou's", it turns out that, as a very young child, Melinda Lou had trouble pronouncing her own name.

Instead of saying "Melinda" she would say, "Wenda", and as a result, the family affectionately nicknamed her...*Wendy*.

And that's how Dave Thomas and *Wendy's* came to be the third largest hamburger chain in the world.

A Railroad Story

Ever since I was a kid, I have loved trains. I like songs about trains, movies about trains; I like model trains. A couple of summers ago I was driving up U.S. Highway 85 toward Greeley, Colorado and dozens of cars were pulled over on the side of the road. I didn't have any idea what they were doing, but I thought I'd pullover too just to see. About two minutes later, the big *Union Pacific 3985* steam locomotive came barreling down the tracks at sixty miles per hour and it was something to behold. The smoke, the soot, the noise, the ground shaking beneath your feet. If this monster doesn't get your heart pumping, have a friend call the undertaker because you're dead.

There's something especially romantic about passenger train travel, and a lot of really good movies have trains in them. Movies like *Strangers on a Train* or *Silver Streak* or *North by Northwest* come to mind. Unfortunately, passenger trains have pretty much gone the way of the dodo bird since the construction of the interstate highway system, which means that, for the most part, trains are mainly used for hauling freight.

Norfolk Southern's advertising claims that it can haul a ton of just about anything more than 400 miles on a single gallon of diesel fuel. I'm sure they have their numbers right. After all, once you get a train rolling it will coast from here to the next county. Trains have so much energy in them that our language is full of expressions that make the point.

Expressions like, *a runaway train*, Or being *railroaded*.

Since we're on the subject of railroad expressions:

If you're *on a roll,* you just keep going until you lose your, *train of thought* or maybe you get, *sidetracked*. Of course the opposite of sidetracked is, *fast tracked*, which means you've got *the green light* to move with a *full head of steam*, another railroad expression.

While I'm at it. Red-for-stop and green-for-go both come from the railroads. That turned out to be a bad choice of colors, because most of the people who are color-blind, actually aren't color-blind at all; they just can't tell the difference between, you guessed it, red and green.

Here's a really cool word, if you're into really cool words. The word *"sabotage"* comes from the French word, *Sabot*. In French, *sabot* means clog or shoe, and refers to the metal 'shoe' that holds the railroad track onto the tie. So, when union workers in France wanted more money, they would derail trains by knocking out the metal shoe, or *sabot*, that held the rails together, and the people who did that were called, *"saboteurs."*

I don't want you to think that I have a *"one track"* mind here, but another fun railroad term is, *"hell on wheels"*; which originated during the construction of the trans-continental railroad. The work crews labored under such miserable conditions that they considered it to be a form of hell, and since the whole operation never stayed in once place longer than it took to lay more track, whatever town was at the temporary end of the line became known as, *Hell on Wheels*.

Here's some more fun stuff.

The old-time baseball pitching great, Walter Johnson, was nicknamed, *the Big Train,* because his fastball was said to have roared by batters like a locomotive. You just stood back and watched it go by. By the way, there was a pro-football player named Dick *"Night Train"* Lane who played for the Los Angeles Rams. He was a defensive back, and I wish I could tell you he got his name from crashing into opposing players like a train in the night, but it isn't so. *Night Train Lane* was afraid of flying and would catch up with the rest of the team by traveling overnight on the railroad.

Okay, better *get back on track.*

The hardest thing about operating a train is getting it to stop. I mean, think about this: the locomotive on a modern diesel can weigh up to a million pounds. Add a hundred coal cars, each weighing about 110 tons and you have a payload of about twenty-two million pounds rolling down the mainline at seventy miles an hour. That's why it takes a freight train better than a mile to stop.

In the old days, all trains were slowed down in two ways: first, the engineer would put the engine into reverse and that would help, and then, second, a guy known as the brakeman would turn a big mechanical wheel on the railway cars and apply a set of mechanical brakes. The bad news is that each car had its own set of brakes and if you had a big train, you were going to need a lot of brakemen. Railroads didn't like to pay for a lot of brakemen and until the late 1860's a lot of trains crashed and a lot of people got killed.

But, in 1869, a young man from the town of Central Bridge, New York invented a safety device that made him a fortune and saved countless lives in the process. His name was George Westinghouse, and the device that he invented is still in use today, pretty much as originally envisioned. It's called, the air brake.

Now, air brakes do two things: first they use compressed air to activate <u>all</u> the brakes on a train at the same time. That made it a whole lot easier to stop a train, although it did put a lot of those brakemen out of work. Secondly, air brakes are *fail-safe*. All the brakes in the system are connected by a high-pressure hose. If the hose gets disconnected or ruptured, all the air pressure is lost and the brakes apply automatically.

Nowadays, we take this sort of thing for granted, but back in the days when Rutherford B. Hayes was President, this was a very big deal, and the air brake made Westinghouse very wealthy. Wealthy enough that he was able to turn his attention to even bigger and better projects. In fact, every time you turn on a light switch, you can thank George Westinghouse.

That's because, with the money he made from the air brake and a couple of other nifty inventions, he was able to finance Nikola Tesla and the development of a form of electricity called *alternating current*, or *AC*. This was much to the chagrin of another inventor, Thomas Edison, who had bet most of his chips on a form of electricity called, *direct current* or *DC*. The reason that AC is the standard of the world is because it can be transmitted over hundreds of miles. DC, on the other hand, can only be transmitted over short distances, which means you would have had to put a power plant on every street corner; something that Thomas Edison wanted. As an aside, Edison so despised the competition from alternating current that he went to considerable lengths to discredit the technology.

Anyway, The Westinghouse Corporation, still exists, principally in the power generating business having been responsible for making much of the electrification of America possible. The company even built the original hydro-electric power generating station at Niagara Falls, New York.

It's the same company whose refrigerators, televisions and other appliances were a mainstay of American households in the 1950's and 60's, long after anybody could remember its connection to the railroads or air brakes. A company that started with one young entrepreneur who saw a need, filled it, made himself rich in the process, and made every passenger and freight train in the world much safer. A company whose advertising slogan is known worldwide...

"You can be sure....if it's... Westinghouse"

Of Arms and Men

This story begins with an inventor that you have probably never heard of, and finishes with a few names that everybody has heard of, and a rifle known as, *the gun that won the West.* But first, a little background.

It is often said that the military is always fighting the last war. Of course, the critique begs the question; what other war should they be fighting?

I mean, if you think about it, if you were victorious in the last war, it only makes sense to prepare for the same thing again. Unless there is a change in the actual technology of warfare, you can pretty much assume that next year's battle will be a lot like this year's or last year's. And, in fact, it is technological change that has marked the major milestones of military history.

The invention of the stirrup by the Chinese created cavalry and allowed a force of a hundred riders to defeat an army of a thousand foot soldiers. By the way, in case you've never been out of the city, the stirrup is what you put your feet in when riding a horse. As another example, the crossbow increased the carnage on the battlefields to the point that Pope Innocent II condemned it as being inhumane.

The truth is, armies might still be hacking and stabbing at each other with clubs, swords, spears and crossbows had it not been for something that happened almost entirely by accident.

Sometime around the 7th century A.D., chemists in China started looking for what they hoped would be "the Elixir of Life," sort of the fountain of youth in a bottle. For the record, they didn't find what they were looking for, but you've got to hand it to them for their persistence. For about three hundred years, they came up with one concoction after another; all sorts of combinations of things, mostly poisonous, that they were sure would bring eternal life. They ground up jade, gold, arsenic, mercury. You name it and they ground it up and drank it. Too bad they didn't have warning labels back in those days, they could have saved a bundle on funeral expenses. They never found what they were looking for, but somewhere around the 9th century they came up with a little bit of chemistry that made quite a bang, literally. It was the combination of sulfur, charcoal and saltpeter that we know as, gunpowder. Of course, they didn't call it gunpowder at the time because nobody had any guns.

In fact, the Chinese didn't really know what to do with the new magic powder, but they discovered if you set a fire to it, it would create a tremendous flash and a bang, which marked the beginning of fireworks.

Now, fireworks are a lot of fun, but they're not much good on a battlefield, and in the middle twelve hundreds, the Arabs came up with a better idea. They put a load of the Chinese magic powder into a bronze pipe, filled the pipe with rocks, sealed up one end of the thing, put a match to it and, kaboom...the military world was in the cannon business. It was so effective that the Arabs used their new cannon to take over the city of Constantinople, which immediately went from being Christian to Muslim in the process, and is why we now call it Istanbul.

The cannon started a serious arms race. Everybody wanted one. After all, nobody wants to be the last guy on the block to have a cannon. It pretty much spelled the end of things like the catapult and the trebuchet. They were pretty effective in their day, but a heck of a hassle to move around. The cannon was in for good, and it wasn't too long before somebody came up with the idea of a hand-held cannon. It was basically a long tube, filled with projectiles, that you pointed at somebody you didn't like. Now, you could do some real damage. After a couple of hundred years, the hand cannon evolved into the musket, and that was pretty much the state of firearms until shortly before the American Civil War.

If you've ever seen one, it becomes obvious that the musket is a pretty clumsy contraption. You have to pour some gunpowder down the barrel, pack it down a little bit, roll a lead ball down after it, take aim at your target and squeeze off a round, usually while somebody else is shooting at you. If you were skilled, you could probably get off a shot a minute.

In the mid 1500's somebody had the idea to pre-package the gunpowder into little envelopes, which sped up the process quite a bit. With that breakthrough, you might be able to squeeze off three shots a minute. Nobody knows who had the idea first; my guess is that it was somebody who was pretty tired of being shot at.

Then, in 1848, a guy you've probably never heard of named Walter Hunt, had an idea that really improved the musket; it was a better kind of ammunition called, the *rocket ball*. The rocket ball was somewhat misnamed in that it was not spherical as the name suggests. It was a modern-looking bullet that was hollow on the backside and filled with gunpowder. Just drop one down the barrel, pull the trigger and bang...you're a shooting machine! It seems so obvious now, but nobody had thought of it before Hunt and it changed the way guns were made.

After inventing the rocket ball, Walter Hunt had an even better idea; take a bunch of rocket balls, stack them in a tube and use a lever to load them into the gun barrel. You could now fire shots about as fast as you could work the lever. He called his new invention *the Volition Rifle*. It was the world's first <u>repeating</u> rifle, and it revolutionized firearms, but it had all sorts of mechanical problems.

In fact, the Volition Rifle had so many problems that a couple of Connecticut gun makers named Horace Smith and Daniel Wesson decided to try to improve it. You're probably thinking this is the Smith and Wesson story, but it's not quite. Smith and Wesson made a few changes to the Volition Rifle and called their improved version *the Volcanic Rifle*. It was clearly an improvement, but still had some problems.

The problems with the Volcanic Rifle would eventually be solved, but unfortunately for Smith and Wesson, in the short run their biggest problem was money. While they were very good at making guns, they weren't all that good at running a business, and in 1850 when their company found itself in financial trouble they sought help from outside investors.

That was when a Connecticut clothing manufacturer decided to get into the firearms business. Over the next few years, he bailed out Smith and Wesson, bought the rights to make the Volcanic Rifle and started a company he called the *New Haven Arms Company*. But the best thing he got in the deal was a great gun maker by the name of, Benjamin Tyler Henry, and it was Henry who actually perfected the repeating rifle.

Henry's improvement was called, the *Henry Rifle*, and is <u>almost</u> the most famous rifle in history, because it was better than both the Volition and Volcanic rifles, made the musket completely obsolete and helped the Union Army defeat the Confederates in the Civil War. The Confederates cursed the Henry Rifles and called them, *"Sunday Rifles,"* because you could *"load 'em on Sunday and keep shooting for the rest of the week."* The Henry was so good that Union soldiers actually paid for them out of their own pockets. They had to; the musket was still the <u>official</u> weapon of the Army, since that's what they'd used in the last war. If you wanted a Henry, you had to pay for it. Crazy how it works, isn't it?

You can still buy a Henry rifle today, but the most famous rifle of all time is an improved version that's named after the Connecticut clothing manufacturer who ponied up all the money. There's even a famous Jimmy Stewart movie western about it; the rifle that bears the name of that Connecticut businessman who got out of making clothing, bailed out Smith and Wesson and got into making firearms; a man by the name of...

Oliver <u>Winchester,</u>

whose *Winchester model 1873* is known as, "the gun that won the west."

America's Pastime

Today's story is really a baseball story, but I'm going to throw you quite a few curves, before we get to the end.

The other day I was looking for something to help eliminate the tartar and bad breath that my little dog, Marty, has from time to time. Well, most of the time. It turns out that while it's possible to brush a dog's teeth, only the veterinarian should handle the job, and it'll cost you about two hundred bucks. This led me on an odyssey that began with a Google search, and eventually ended up in the doggie treat isle of the super-market, where I bought a box of Milk Bones for about five bucks. They seem to do the trick, Marty loves them and I'm a hundred and ninety-five dollars in the clear.

This got me to wondering about how <u>people</u> must have cleaned their teeth thousands of years ago, before there was a store-full of toothbrushes and a complete range of things you can put into your mouth to handle the job. The first actual tooth cleaning device was apparently created about three thousand years ago. It was called the chewing stick, and that pretty much describes the thing. It was a stick, and you chewed on it. Somebody could have probably made a lot of money copyrighting the name, *chewing stick*, but nobody ever did, although I understand that Al Gore's ancestors had a hand in the development.

Before the invention of the chewing stick, people pretty much had to improvise, and it appears that we chewed on all sorts of things, including the bark of trees, and that is really where our story begins.

Since about 5,000 B.C., people have been chewing on tree bark as both a way of scraping the plaque buildup off their teeth, and for medicinal reasons as well. For example, the Romans discovered that the bark of the white willow tree contains the basic ingredients of what we call aspirin.

But I suspect that the real reason people chew things is that we just like the sensation of chewing. People chew, gum, tobacco, straw; we chew on our shirts, our hair, the ends of pens and pencils. We chew on our glasses, our fingernails, paperclips, rubber bands, toothpicks; you name and somebody will chew on it.

Sigmund Freud said that all that chewing was related to an oral obsession that goes back to our infancy. I think Freud had a couple of obsessions of his own.

I'm not sure if people 5,000 years ago had enough time on their hands to have oral obsessions, but whatever the reason, we, along with pretty much the rest of the animal kingdom, live in a world of chewers, and ever since we stopped gnawing on trees, by far the most popular thing to chew has been...chewing gum.

There are all kinds of chewing gums; ball gum, stick gum, string gum, bubble gum, gum with a candy center. There's even caffeinated gum that they give to soldiers to help them stay awake while they're on duty. I'm thinking of sending a case to Congress.

So, where does all this gum come from anyway? Well, for the most part it comes from the sap of trees. Somebody must have figured that out while they were chomping on all that bark. Frankincense, the same stuff mentioned in the Bible, comes from the sap of the Boswellia tree and was a popular chew back in the time of the Pharaohs. When Europeans first came to the New world, they discovered that the natives liked to chew on the sap from pine trees.

The ancient Greeks chewed on a resin from the Mastic Tree. Today, the word mastic refers to that adhesive you use to set ceramic tiles on the floor. The original probably didn't taste much better.

In 1848, a guy named, John Curtis, started selling what he called, The State of Maine Pure Spruce Gum." It probably made a pretty good chew, if you like the taste of Pine Sol. Modern chewing gum originally came from something called, *chicle*, which was chewed by the Aztecs. The chewing gum, "Chiclets," gets its name form chicle. Chicle was actually first considered as a possible rubber substitute. Unfortunately, it's not much good as rubber, but it makes a pretty darn good gum. Now they use <u>artificial</u> chicle because the real stuff is too expensive.

By the 1870's, chewing gum was starting to become big business, as was the next part of our story, professional baseball. Around 1870, baseball, which for the most part had been an amateur sport, went professional. The first professional team was the *Cincinnati Red Stockings*. Soon after that, a team was formed that called itself the *Chicago White Stockings*. The White Stockings would go through a couple of name changes, the last of which came in 1902 when the new owner, a guy named Jim Hart, decided to call them the *Chicago Cubs*.

Everything went well for major League Baseball until 1914 when a newly formed league, the Federal League, decided to compete for fans and stole players from the existing National and American Leagues. One of the teams in the new Federal league called itself the *Chicago Whales*. It was started by a guy named Charles Weehgman, who had made a pile of dough setting up lunch counters all over Chicago. He also built a beautiful new ball park on the North side of Chicago, which he called, Weeghman Park...ownership has its privileges.

Well, in 1916, two years after getting started, the Federal League went bankrupt, but Weeghman landed on his feet. That's because yet another new owner of the Cubs, a guy named Albert Lasker was looking for a partner with money. (He's the same Albert Lasker who is generally considered the father of modern advertising) Oh, and it would be nice if the new partner owned a baseball park, too.

So now, Lasker and Weeghman owned the Chicago Cubs, and the team played at Weeghman Park. But they didn't own the <u>whole</u> club. They had a couple of minority shareholders. One of them was a guy who had started a business in 1891 selling soap and baking soda. Apparently, baking soda sales were only so so back in the "Gay Nineties", so our baking soda entrepreneur decided to see if he could spark things up by putting a little something into each can that was sold. And that little something was a stick of, guess what?

Chewing gum!

Boy, did that ever spruce things up! The more gum in the can, the more cans they sold and pretty soon the company got out of the baking soda business and into the chewing gum business. The owner of that company was a guy named, William Wrigley, Jr., whose name is synonymous with things like, Juicy Fruit, Spearmint, Doublemint, and Big Red to name just a few.

By 1925, Wrigley had made so much money selling Juicy Fruit and Doublemint that he bought out Weeghman and Lasker, and he and the Wrigley family became the sole owners of the Cubs; an honor they enjoyed for almost sixty years.

In 1981, they sold the team and the ballpark to the company that owned The Chicago Tribune, The Tribune Company, which went broke and sold the team and the ballpark to a real estate tycoon by the name of Sam Zell. Zell sold it all to the founder of a company called *Ameritrade*, a guy named Tom Ricketts, who owns it all today but still calls the team the Cubs; who still play on the north side of Chicago at a place called *Wrigley Field*, that got its name in 1925 from a guy who started out selling cans of baking soda with a stick of gum inside. A man named...*William Wrigley*.

Things remembered

The following stories aren't related to any specific company, but they make for entertaining reading. They are the stories behind the stories we all know.

Iceberg

If you have ever been to the campus of Harvard University, among the many striking buildings that adorn the grounds is the Harry Elkins Widener Memorial Library; a magnificent edifice that houses over fifty miles of bookshelves, with a capacity to hold some 3 million volumes.

It was a gift to Harvard by a grief-stricken mother in loving memory of her son, a Harvard Graduate and book collector whose life was cut short in one of the greatest disasters ever to take place at sea; a tragedy that took the lives of the industrialist Benjamin Guggenheim, the millionaire John Jacob Astor IV, Macy's Department store owner Isidor Strauss, his wife Ida and some fifteen hundred others in the early morning hours of the fifteenth of April, Nineteen Hundred and Twelve.

By any measure, the year 1912 was going to be an exceptional one. The world was fully into the new twentieth century and was quickly shrinking. The Republic of China was established. New Mexico and Arizona were admitted to the Union as the forty-seventh and forty-eighth States. The expedition of Robert F. Scott had reached the South pole, only to discover, sadly, that the Norwegian Roald Amundsen had arrived there a month earlier. In Boston, Fenway Park was opened to the public for the first time. The light bulb had replaced the gas lamps of the nineteenth century. The telephone, the telegraph, and newly invented wireless telegraphy had ushered-in a communications revolution. The world had changed, and with it, mankind had developed a new sense of the possible.

The limitations of all of the previous chapters of recorded history were quickly disappearing. The automobile was rapidly replacing the horse and buggy. The great wooden sailing vessels of the previous era had been replaced by floating seagoing islands, made of iron and powered by steam. Ships of immense size and proportion now carried passengers over the once harrowing voyage of the North Atlantic in a matter of mere days, in splendor and comfort that was once only a dream.

And it would be one of those ships that would make tragic history; a disaster so memorable that there have been no fewer than eight motion pictures dedicated to its fateful maiden voyage, and nearly three times that many films have featured the doomed ship in one way or another.

It was the second of three sister ships commissioned by the White Star Line, built at the Harland and Wolfe shipyard in Belfast in Northern Ireland and financed by the American, J.P. Morgan. The older sister of the trio had been launched a year earlier and given the name *Olympic*. The last of the three would be christened *Britannic*. Powered by three steam-driven engines that produced a combined 46,000 horsepower, the ship, displacing just over fifty-two thousand tons, was as majestic as anything that has ever sailed upon the sea; a living monument to the genius of engineering.

With its designation R.M.S. or *Royal Mail Ship*, she left her berth in Southampton on the southern coast of England at ten in the morning on Wednesday, April 10th. On board were some 2,278 passengers and crew, well below the ships capacity of 3,400, but also well in excess of the carrying capacity of the scant twenty lifeboats that had been placed aboard. It was a ship that had been thought to be unsinkable because of a system of watertight doors that could be closed to seal the ship's lower compartments in the event of a disaster. For the record, the system failed.

The only thing that was unsinkable about the great White Star Liner was one of the passengers who boarded at Cherbourg on the coast of France; a forty-six year old woman from Denver, originally named Margaret Tobin, who had married the silver miner, James J. Brown. After living in near poverty for many years of marriage, the Browns would finally strike it rich in the mountains near Leadville, Colorado, and Mrs. Brown was treating herself to something special. While she was alive, her friends called her, Maggie, but historians would later dub her the Unsinkable Molly Brown out of respect to her hardheaded but futile efforts to rescue fellow passengers. From Cherbourg, the ship would sail to Queenstown in Ireland and finally set sail on its maiden voyage to New York.

By all accounts, the voyage was a vision of perfection; a sleek, crisp white-over-black mass of architectural beauty cutting its way through the deep blue of the North Atlantic ocean. Sailing effortlessly into the moonless night of Sunday, April 14, the ship's lookouts, Frederick Fleet and Reginald Lee, stood watch in the crow's nest. The ship's clock had just struck seven bells, 11:30 in the evening, thirty minutes before a crew change. Ten minutes later and roughly four hundred miles south of Newfoundland, they would see a monster, barely visible in the dark of the night; a mountain of ice directly in the ship's path. A quick call to the bridge would say all that needed to be said, "iceberg, right ahead."

Desperately, First Officer William Murdoch ordered the ship to steer to the left.

They almost made it.

The great vessel avoided a direct collision, barely grazing the jagged edge of the iceberg that left a two hundred ninety foot gash below the waterline. Of course, the rest is history. Two and a half hours later, the ship that was deemed unsinkable would slip below the waves and come to rest some twelve thousand feet below the surface. Of the over twenty-two hundred souls on board, only seven hundred and six would survive.

Which brings us full circle, back to the Widener Library at Harvard, where you will find the simple dedication to the young man after whom it was named. It reads:

Harry Elkins Widener, a graduate of this University, born January 3, 1885, died at sea, April 15, 1912 upon the foundering of the steamship...

Titanic.

The Flying Lumberyard

If you have ever been to Long Beach, California, you have had the opportunity to visit something truly remarkable. One of the great monuments to the science of shipbuilding sits in the harbor, parked in a permanent mooring, far from its original home. It is the luxury liner, *The Queen Mary*; the magnificent thousand foot steamship that was the pride of the Cunard Company from the day of her maiden voyage in 1936.

I have had the pleasure of having cocktails in the *Observation Bar* on the Queen Mary and it is well worth the trip. But if you had the pleasure of seeing the Queen Mary before 1992, you will find that something is now missing in the city of Long Beach. It is one of the aeronautical wonders of the world which used to be located within a stone's throw of the Queen.

It is probably the most controversial airplane that was ever built; the subject of scorn, ridicule, admiration, a Senate hearing and the subject of today's story.

 One of the largest moving projects in the history of the west coast involved the dismantling of an airplane, placing it on a barge, towing it from the southern coast of California and then finally transporting it, piece by piece, on semi-trailer trucks to its final resting place at the Evergreen Aviation and Space Museum, about sixty miles south of Portland, Oregon. It was an undertaking that took place over the span of one hundred and thirty eight days, beginning in October of 1992 and ending at the end of February of 1993.

It was the end point of a journey that really began decades earlier, in the middle of World War II, when the great industrialist Henry Kaiser had an idea to build the largest troop carrier ever conceived. Kaiser, if you don't know the story, was a production genius whose skills at mass production were unparalleled during the War.

It was Kaiser who is most famous for the production of the *Liberty Ships*, the mass-produced cargo carriers that literally kept the lifeline of men and material alive between the United States and Great Britain. They weren't pretty, but they were cheap, and America turned out just over twenty-seven hundred of them during the course of the war. The production was so efficient, that one ship, *The Robert E. Peary,* was built in less than five days from stem to stern.

But the human toll on the Merchant Marines who manned the Liberty ships was fearsome. German U-boat Wolf packs routinely sank the slow-sailing boats with alarming regularity. Fortunately, the production was so prolific that the Nazi's couldn't keep up.

Still, wartime has a way of engendering new solutions to old problems. In 1942, Henry Kaiser commissioned the Hughes Aircraft Corporation to build a prototype flying boat; a sea-based airplane that could carry 750 fully-loaded soldiers and one Sherman tank across the Atlantic ocean. It was a massive endeavor that would create the largest plane ever flown. It was originally called the HK-1; a reference to the partnership between Henry Kaiser and Howard Hughes, but its official designation would later be the *H-4 Hercules.*

Its wingspan was three hundred and thirty feet, slightly more than the length of a football field. To give some perspective, the Wright brother's first flight off the sand hills of Kitty Hawk, North Carolina could have actually taken off, flown and landed on on either wing of the Hercules.

Because of a lack of aluminum to create this massive airplane, something altogether different was conceived. It was to be built out of a composite of what is basically plywood; a construction of mostly birch wood laminates that would be not only light, but also strong enough to handle the engineering demands of so mammoth an airplane.

Being made of wood, the plane was often called "the flying lumberyard" and would later be dubbed with the nickname by which it is known today; a name that Howard Hughes bitterly resented. It was regularly ridiculed by critics for its size, construction materials and production delays, and, in fact, was not completed until well after the war had ended.

After the war, the plane was the focus of a bitter Senate hearing on wartime appropriations headed by Maine Senator, Ralph Owen Brewster, a staunch conservative and a man whom Hughes accused of being an errand boy for the head of Pan American World Airways' chairman, Juan Trippe.

Trippe and Howard Hughes were in competition to secure aviation rights for commercial overseas passenger service. Senator Brewster had sponsored a bill that would have given Pan American the exclusive monopoly at the expense of Hugh's rival, *Trans World Airlines* or TWA. The stage was set for a confrontation.

During a Senate hearing, on August 6, 1947, in the first of a number of appearances, Hughes put his reputation on the line when he said:

"The Hercules was a monumental undertaking. It is the largest aircraft ever built. It is over five stories tall with a wingspan longer than a football field. That's more than a city block. Now, I put the sweat of my life into this thing. I have my reputation all rolled up in it, and I have stated several times that if it's a failure I'll probably leave this country and never come back. And I mean it."

Hughes, was not about to leave the country and was not about to be proven a failure or a fool.

And so it was, that on November 2, 1947, the industrialist and aviation pioneer who had staked his reputation on this project, climbed into the cockpit of this wooden plane along with thirty-one others, powered up the eight 4,000 horsepower Pratt and Whitney engines and took the behemoth for a series of test runs near Long Beach. During one of those runs, Hughes pushed the throttles forward and, within a few minutes, the one hundred and fifty ton Hercules lifted off the water and became airborne. The flight lasted for less than a minute and traveled just over a mile before gently settling back down on the water.

It would be the first and last flight of the Hercules...the flying boat built of <u>birch</u> wood laminate...that almost from its very beginning was incorrectly nicknamed....*The* <u>*Spruce*</u> *Goose.*

October Skies

On July 29, 1955, President Dwight Eisenhower, through his press secretary, James Hagerty, let it be known that the United States planned to launch a satellite to orbit the Earth in 1957, during the much heralded International Geophysical Year. Whether he realized it or not, Eisenhower had thrown down the gauntlet. A date with destiny had been set, and much to our horror in the middle of the cold war, the Russians beat us to the punch.

If you look up into the night sky, far away from the city lights, you can see the reflection of thousands of pieces of space debris floating above the earth. There's almost no end to the stuff. Aside from dead satellites and rocket boosters, there are wrenches, gloves, a couple of high end cameras and garbage bags; it's a virtual junkyard up there. Fortunately, most space junk floats around in the same direction, kind of like kids at the roller rink, otherwise things would start running into each other and raining down on us poor earthlings like something from a bad science-fiction movie. But there was a time, not all that long ago, when there was nothing in space but...well...space.

While rockets have been around for a couple of thousand years, dating back to the ancient Chinese, the first attempt to get off the planet by man is generally thought to have happened just a few hundred years ago, with the unsuccessful, let's call it *"launch"* of the would be Chinese Astronaut, Wan-Hu, in the early sixteenth century.

According to the American author, Herbert Zim, Wan sat in a chair to which some forty-seven rockets had been attached. A team of assistants lit the rockets, and the whole thing...exploded. After the smoke cleared, both Wan and the rocket chair had disappeared. He may not have made it into orbit, but Wan certainly left this world...and with a bang.

It probably wouldn't have worked anyway; there's not enough energy in gunpowder to slip what John Gillespie Magee famously called, *"the surly bonds of Earth."* A few centuries after Wan, the American, Dr. Robert Goddard figured out how to create a lot more thrust with liquid propellants, and laid the groundwork for the modern age of rocketry.

Two people who had shown a keen interest in Goddard's work were the German scientist, Wernher von Braun, and an aspiring Soviet aircraft designer named, Sergei Korolyev. Von Braun, as most people know, would go on to develop the V-2 rocket program with which Adolf Hitler had planned to destroy England in World War II. Toward the end of the war, von Braun and many fellow Germans would surrender to American authorities and would use their knowledge to help develop the American space program. The Soviets, too, would acquire their own hoard of displaced German scientists.

Sergei Korolyev, met with a different fate. In 1938, he was imprisoned for misuse of funds in a trumped up charge that had been part of Joseph Stalin's *Great Purge*, the mindless program of almost random executions and imprisonments that gutted the Soviet military and scientific community of its best talent, virtually on the eve of the second World War. It turns out that Korolyev had been spending state money on rocket research, something Stalin could undoubtedly have used against Hitler. After six years of torture, and imprisonment, Korolyev was finally released and allowed to work on...what else...rockets, and would go on to be known as the father of the Soviet Space program.

After the end of the War, Korolyev set out to create something that eventually changed the world. It was the refinement of the intercontinental ballistic missile or ICBM, that had been pioneered by Wernher von Braun.

   The ICBM changed the face of modern warfare. With both the U.S. and the Soviets in possession of nuclear weapons, the question became how to deliver them. Long-range bombers have to be refueled in mid-air and are vulnerable to numerous defensive countermeasures. But the ICBM is a completely different kind of threat; a faceless menace that is simply launched about hundred miles into space and then falls back to Earth to rain unspeakable destruction onto the enemy below.

By the mid 1950's, it was no secret that both sides of the Cold War were working on reliable missile programs; but the devil is in the details. It's one thing to set off a rocket, it's something entirely different to launch one that will come down pretty close to where you want it. After all, you don't want an armed nuke dropping just anywhere, especially back in your own back yard. But if you could place an ICBM exactly where you wanted, it would send a clear message to the other side; it would forever change the balance of power.

By the mid 1950's, the space race was on in earnest, and the winner would be able dictate terms to the loser. The stakes had never been higher and both sides knew it.

Then, on October 4th, 1957, the world received a dose of cold hard reality. The Russians, had beaten the technically advanced Americans; putting the first man-made satellite into space. It was a twenty-three inch polished metal sphere that weighed less than 200 pounds, but its weight was felt worldwide; its relentless battery-powered radio pulse suggesting what was once thought impossible; that <u>their</u> Germans were smarter than <u>our</u> Germans. From that day, the world has never been the same.

It happened in the first week of October, 1957 when America woke up to the sound of something new out of the October Sky, the steady chirping of a satellite whose name in Russian means, *"fellow traveler"*, what the rest of us came to know as...

Sputnik.

Too Good To Be True

If Bernie Madoff had been born fifty years earlier, then the world's most notorious investment scheme would probably have been named after him instead of being called a Ponzi scheme. Madoff was certainly the greatest of the Ponzi schemers in terms of dollar volume, having been the mastermind of what has been described as the biggest Ponzi scheme in history. I suppose it would have been only fitting if such a con man had been the father of the systematic theft that either destroyed or crippled so many investors; it almost sounds like a movie title: . *Bernie...the man who made-off with everybody's money.* But, alas, there's no Hollywood ending to the story, at least not yet.

But what exactly is a Ponzi scheme anyway and where did it get its name?

First things first. A Ponzi scheme is an investment swindle where investors are paid so-called *returns*, either out of their own money, or out of money received from new investors. In almost every case, an original group of suckers is drawn into some kind of story that promises fantastic returns on their money, based on some new approach to investing, inside information or any gimmick that gives participants a leg up on the rest of the investment world. Wealth without risk. All gain and no pain.

Now, in order to accomplish this impossible feat, the person setting up the deal has to be one of two things:

A: either he is the greatest investor in the history of the world or
B: he is a thief.

It turns out that *B* is the correct answer. It's a lot easier to be a thief.

The mechanics are really quite simple. You give me, say, ten thousand dollars; a million would be better, but ten grand will have to do for now. I promise to make fifty percent per year on your money for you. Who's going to say "no" to that?

Step two: I need to find another person with ten thousand dollars a few days later and I make her the same promise. Now, all I have to do is write you a check for five thousand with half the money I received from investor number two. You'll think you made fifty percent, and I've just and put the remaining five grand in my pocket. Of course, pretty soon, I'll have to find a third person with ten thousand dollars and then a fourth and a fifth and so on and so on. The new "investors" keep the old investors in the chips, so to speak. It all works out pretty well until I run out of new people who have ten thousand dollars to invest. It reminds me of what Margaret Thatcher said about socialism: it works great until you run out of other people's money.

Of course, like any swindle, there has to be a plausible story. If you've seen the movie, "The Sting", the grifters Henry Gondorf and Johnny Hooker, convince their mark, the gangster Doyle Lonnegan, that they had set up a crooked scheme to delay horse racing results. It was a sure thing. Can't lose. Just put up a little money and wait for the payoff.

Bernie Madoff's story was a little more sophisticated. He convinced his victims that he was dealing in something called *split strike options conversion*. That just sounds cool doesn't it? Too, complicated for the average investor; deal me in. And so it went...to the tune of billions of dollars. After all, if you can't understand it, the guy who can must be a financial genius, right? By the way, Mr. Madoff is scheduled to be released from prison in the year 2159. (I'm not sure of the exact day of release)

The original Ponzi scheme was no different in the sense that new contributors paid for the old, (this is starting to sound a lot like the Social Security System) and there was also a great story behind those easy profits.

Here's how it went.

Around the turn of the century, the 1900's that is, mailing a letter overseas inadvertently created what's known as a *risk-free arbitrage*. An arbitrage is a price difference between two markets and here's the simplified version of how it worked.

Let's say that you wanted to send a letter from America to Europe, you could buy the postage here for say, fifty cents. Then, if you wanted to get a letter back from the foreign country, you could pay another fifty cents in advance for the return postage. One dollar altogether. Still with me? But, if you had bought the return postage in the foreign country, the total cost would have been a little less. To make things easy, we'll say that you could have saved a dime on the whole transaction; meaning that a smart person could charge a dollar for foreign mail delivery and pocket a dime with every letter that was sent overseas. It's actually a little more complicated than that, but not much, and, in any event, it sure makes a good story doesn't it?

Just imagine that every letter sent to grandma back in the old country had the potential of having a free dime attached to it.

With a scheme like that you could promise investors fantastic returns. And that's just what happened. A young Italian immigrant who had come to America penniless, set up shop in New York City. He had come to the land of opportunity, in his own words "with $2.50 in my pocket and a million dollars worth of hope." He told this fantastic story of international postal profits to people who were only too eager to make money for doing nothing. He offered them a whopping forty-five percent return on their money, every ninety days. Who could resist?

Now in fairness, the scheme actually started out as a legitimate enterprise; the young mastermind sent money to relatives in the old country to purchase foreign postage. But when he went to redeem the stamps here for cash, the time and expense of all the red-tape turned out to be more of a hassle than it was worth. But the <u>story</u> still sounded good. After all, it <u>could </u>have worked if somebody had wanted to go to all the trouble. But the young entrepreneur, whose first name was Charles, didn't really have the time or the energy to put all that effort into the task. It was a lot easier to sell the story than do the work.

And, boy, did it sell well! In February of 1920, the "investment company" that Charlie set up pulled in five thousand dollars. By that May, it was pulling in close to a half a million dollars...a month. Honestly, who had the time to buy that many stamps? Nobody did. Within a year, millions had poured in to the scheme.

Sadly, nothing lasts forever.

Suspicious of the mega profits that were pouring in, a financial writer named Clarence Barron, after whom *Barron's* Magazine is named, did some calculating and figured out that if the scheme were legitimate, there would have to be more foreign postage stamps floating around than you could fit into the Grand Canyon. Barron's investigative reporting raised a lot of eyebrows; people started wondering if their money was safe.

Then the worst thing that could happen, finally happened. Somebody wanted his money back...and before you know it there was a run on the company, and just like a house of cards, it all came tumbling down.

Eventually, the mastermind of the enterprise spent a short three and a half years in Federal prison, and after much legal wrangling, finally ended up being deported. But, so skillful a con man was he that the scheme he invented still bears his name today....

a man named, Charles Ponzi, father of...*The Ponzi Scheme.*

Money for Nothing

Has this ever happened to you?

I woke up the other day and checked my email, and to my delight I discovered that a London banker wanted to send me millions of dollars for doing almost nothing. What a way to start the morning. With the exception of a slight hook in my golf swing, all my problems would soon be over. I don't know about you, but I could sure use an extra million or two, especially in a down economy.

Imagine my disappointment when I found out it was all a scam. It reminded me of the time I quit my job because the Publishers' Clearing House envelope said I might have already won ten million dollars. Oh well, life is a journey. At any rate, this is the story of the oldest known confidence game on record; a swindle that stretches back over four hundred years.

First, let's start with the letter that I received in my email.

Dear Sir or Madam

*I am a staff of Natwest Bank London. I am writing following a **oppurtunity** in my office that will be of **imense** benefit to both of us. We discovered an abandoned sum of $22 million Dollars in an account that belongs to one of our foreign customers Late Mr. Morris Thompson **a** American who unfortunately lost his life in the plane crash of Alaska Airlines Flight 261 which crashed on January 31th, 2000 including his wife and only daughter.*

Let's see if we can examine just a couple of items in the letter to see if it's really legit. First, the words *immense* and *opportunity* were both misspelled. I mention this fact simply to point out that one would think that a top ranking officer at a prestigious London Bank might have achieved the academic skills to pass third grade spelling, or at the very least, that the bank could afford a word processing program with a spell-checker. The writer also had some trouble with the use of the articles, 'a','an' and 'the'. English does have its little quirks.

Anyway, the letter goes on to tell me that since there are no legitimate heirs to Mr. Thompson's twenty-two million dollars, I can pretty well have most of it as long as I send a small fee for shipping and handling. Gee, I wonder if that's where the late night kitchen gadget and weight loss promoters got the idea for the shipping and handling fee.

My email was signed by a bank officer named, Mr. Crawford Leeds. How terribly British indeed! Who is going to argue with a name like that. All I have to do is fork over three hundred dollars, and I can have the twenty-two million.

How cool! I'm just three hundred smackers away from being rich beyond my wildest dreams! I'm not sure how I ended up on the late Morris Thompson's bucket list, but, hey, who cares? This is no time to ask questions. Now's the time to get out the checkbook and wait for the twenty-two million to show up in my bank account.

Of course, I do have one lingering question: Why can't they just roll the three hundred dollar fee in to the jackpot and deduct it from the twenty-two million? I mean Twenty-two million minus three hundred is less than a rounding error. If I re-finance my home loan, they don't need any cash. What gives?

Well, of course, the whole thing is a scam and, sadly, tens of thousands of people have been taken in by this swindle ever since it was first played. It is so engrained in the history of swindles that it has its own name. There was even a movie made about it starring Steve Martin and Campbell Scott.

There are other variations on the story; it can be a lost lottery ticket, or a tax error. In earlier times, a beautiful princess was said to be locked away in a castle somewhere, and if she could only get her hands on a couple of hundred dollars, she would gladly fork over a treasure chest filled with jewels and who knows what else. The most popular modern version has to do with a Nigerian customs agent who has a boatload of gold or silver or unclaimed booty of some kind; for all I know it could be a warehouse full of abandoned hula hoops, that can be redeemed for millions of dollars for the price of a nominal advanced fee.

Now, the original version, and this is where the name of the scam comes from, goes back to the reign of Queen Elizabeth I of England. England and Spain were at odds with one another during the late 16th century and the scam went like this: a con-man approaches a potential victim with a story that the Spanish King, Phillip II, has put a wealthy Englishman in jail for who knows what. They didn't really need a reason back then. The imprisoned Englishman is very wealthy and will gladly pay a large ransom to anyone who secures his release. The sucker has to put up enough money to bribe a guard who has the keys to the dungeon. Just put up a couple of hundred pounds and, in a few weeks, you'll be living on easy street. Of course, there is no fortune and the victim is soon left empty-handed, while the grifter and his colleagues sit around drinking Madeira wine on the Costa del Sol.

It's amazing that so many people have fallen for this scam. After all, why doesn't the princess or the Englishman or somebody between here and Timbuktu just bribe the guard and be done with it? But the hoax lives on today, and while the story may change from time to time, it is always known by the name that it was originally called...a centuries old fraud known as....

The Spanish Prisoner.

The Monster

(recorded October 29, 2010)

Since this is the last *"What's in a Name"* before Halloween, I thought I'd have a little fun and talk about something scary. And, no, I'm not talking about the upcoming mid-term elections, which are just about guaranteed to scare close to half the population regardless of political preference. I sometimes wonder what the founders were thinking when they picked the first Tuesday in November for elections.

Anyway, let's get right down to a quick review of Halloween, although most of you probably know some or most of it, and then we can talk about one of the perennial favorite monsters for the holiday and a little bit of the quirky fun that is associated with him...or it..or..well never mind.

As most of you know, *Halloween*, got its name from the fact that November First is what is known in the Roman Catholic Church as, "All Saints' Day." sometimes called "All Souls Day" or more specifically, "All Hallows" Day. Throw a little bit of a Scottish brogue into the mix, and it isn't much of a stretch to go from *All Hallows Evening* to... Halloween.

But that isn't why we dress up as ghouls and goblins, skeletons, Spider-man, Dracula or Frankenstein. The reason we do that is because of the Celtic Celebration of *Samhain*, which is Gaelic for the *End of Summer*. The Celts believed that autumn, with its falling leaves, dying plant life and other signs of the end of the cycle of life, was a time when the boundary between this world and the world of the afterlife was very thin and that some spirits had the power to come back into the world of the living. The Celts wore masks and other spooky costumes to appease the spirits and keep them on, "the other side."

Okay, so much for the history of Halloween. Now let's have some fun and pick a monster costume...

In 1815, a volcano in Indonesia called *Mount Tambora* exploded, resulting in the largest injection of volcanic ash into the earth's atmosphere in some sixteen hundred years. It happened at a time when sunspot activity was already at a low, and the combination of a cooler sun and a few million tons of volcanic ash led to what became known as, "the forgotten Summer"; a time when the planet cooled noticeably and led to crop failures, starvation and other unpleasant side effects.

One of the side effects was that an aspiring author by the name of Mary Godwin, who was just eighteen at the time, was cooped up most of the summer at the Swiss Villa where her lover and later husband, the English romantic poet Percy Shelley, were staying with fellow writer, Lord Byron. They were all cooped-up because the weather was so bad at lake Geneva, where they were staying, that it rained all the time and there wasn't much to do outside except get wet.

So what did they do? Percy and Mary and their literary buddies sat around the fireplace in the middle of the summer and tried to see if they could scare the willies out of each other with ghost stories. It turned out that the best of the stories came from the teenager, Mary Godwin, who would later become Mary Shelley.

Mary's story was based on an idea that was fairly popular at the time, and it was based on experiments by an Italian scientist named, Luigi Galvani. Galvani is famous because, after Benjamin Franklin had nearly electrocuted himself flying a kite in a thunderstorm, the whole world was fascinated by electricity. And, as one thing leads to another, Luigi

Galvani decided it might be interesting to see what would happen to dead animals if you ran a little bit of electric current through them. Galvani discovered that a little juice in the old road kill would actually get their muscles to twitch. The principle is called *Galvanism*.

Anyway, little miss Mary decided to cook up a story about a scientist who brings a dead man back to life by running a few thousand volts of electricity through him. The name of the scientist in her story was Doctor Victor Frankenstein. Mary Shelley would go on to have the story formalized as a novel and it's called, *"Frankenstein, or the Modern Prometheus."* The book was published in 1818, first anonymously, and then under the author's name, Mary Shelley, and if you've ever seen the Kenneth Branagh film, *Mary Shelley's Frankenstein*, now you know where the title comes from.

But we're not quite finished. When the book was first published, all the critics hated it, of course. Apparently, nobody liked it but the public. They ate it up. It is generally considered one of the very first examples of science fiction writing, and as Stephen King, Ray Bradbury and Rod Serling can attest, you'll probably make a heck of a lot more money writing science fiction than Percy Shelley ever made grinding out romantic poetry. But I digress.

The idea of Frankenstein was so popular that Thomas Edison made a movie about the story, right after he invented the motion picture camera. He was a busy guy. By the way, a lot of people think that Frankenstein is the name of the monster. Not so. The monster is simply called, the monster. Which finally brings us to the focus of the story.

In 1931, the Hollywood production company, Universal Pictures, decided they wanted to come up with a new version of *Frankenstein*. After all, Thomas Edison's version was a silent film, and ever since the Warner Brothers had produced "The Jazz Singer" in 1927, the world wanted "talkies."

So, Universal Pictures hired a director named James Whale to direct their version of the story. Whale did such a great job that he would later go on to direct *Bride of Frankenstein* and *The Invisible Man*, to name just a couple of other horror classics..

And, holy Hannah, did the new version of *Frankenstein* turn out well! It scared the daylights out of everybody. What scared them, of course, was the monster. Probably the best monster anybody had ever seen before and maybe ever since. A tall, mindless, menacing, zombie-like creature with a bolt through his neck, a square head and a growl that would make a grown man shiver in fear. To achieve that embodiment of Mary Shelley's vision of horror, Whale searched high and low until he found a demonic-looking British actor who had been working onstage in Canada and specialized in melodramatic roles as villains, and mad scientists. A man who's birth name was actually, William Henry Pratt, but as he would joke in an interview some years later, "you simply can't have a monster named William Henry Pratt"; which is why he changed his name to...

Boris Karloff.

Happy Halloween everybody!

Turkey Day

One of the curious things about history is that it is easily forgotten. George Santayana prophetically wrote that, "those who do not remember the past are condemned to repeat it." One of my favorite admonitions is inscribed over the entrance to the Norlin library at the University of Colorado that, *He who knows only his own generation remains forever a child.*

In mention this on the day before Thanksgiving because for many Americans, myself included, it is all too easy to assume that the way things are have always been so; that the institutions we take for granted have been around for decades and even centuries, not to be tampered with or modified by whim or fancy or political considerations. But that is not the case. And the holiday that we know as Thanksgiving is no exception.

Because the Thanksgiving Holiday we officially celebrate on the 4th Thursday in November is just under seventy years old, having gone through numerous changes over the years.

But why November, and why the forth Thursday in November?

Our story begins on September 6th, 1620, when one hundred and two passengers seeking religious freedom, boarded *The Mayflower* to sail for what they hoped would be the mouth of the Hudson river in New York. They had been granted land in that area, well south of New England, to establish a colony. They had planned to set sail from their home in England much earlier, probably in July of that year, but many impediments, both logistical and financial delayed their departure until late summer.

If you know the Breton Fisherman's prayer, *Oh God, thy sea is so great and my boat is so small,* the voyage of the Mayflower is the embodiment of those words. The crossing was long and deadly. Two of the ship's complement died on the voyage. A third was thrown overboard in the harrowing winds, but managed to snag a rope and pull himself back onto the ship. Prevailing westerly winds and a strong gulf stream current prevented a speedy crossing of the notoriously treacherous Atlantic, and it was fully sixty-six days later when the weary, seasick group of colonists arrived, not on Plymouth rock, but at the tip of Cape Cod, what is now called Provincetown. They dropped anchor on November 11, 1620, a Saturday. The crew and passengers remained aboard ship to observe the Sabbath the next day, and finally set foot on ground on the following Monday.

Well into the fall and desperately short of food, the settlers began to scavenge for supplies and ended up raiding the winter corn supplies of the local natives. A skirmish between Indians and settlers erupted within a couple of days, and the Mayflower set sail again, this time to land at what they called, New Plymouth, an abandoned native American settlement that had been called, Patuxet. This would be home to those who had survived the journey, but the delays had meant that the construction of the first permanent shelters would not take place until just two days before Christmas.

It was an inauspicious beginning. Under-provisioned and sick from scurvy and other diseases, more than half of the Pilgrims died within the first year. Forty-five died in the first winter alone, and by November of 1621, only fifty-three of the original colonists were still alive. And in that November, the survivors of the ordeal celebrated not what they called *"Thanksgiving,"* but rather, a harvest feast, which they enjoyed with native Americans. It should be quickly noted that giving thanks to God was not a *special* occasion for the Pilgrims. It was a daily routine. They were, after all, Puritans, part of a religious movement that had left England to be, in the words of John Winthrop, *"a beacon of religious light in the New World, to build a city upon a hill."*

The first <u>official</u> Thanksgiving would be celebrated two years later in 1623, probably upon the arrival of the return voyage of the Mayflower, that brought new settlers and much needed tools and supplies. But, it is the more secular November harvest feast that we have come to celebrate as the traditional Thanksgiving. A feast of turkey, breads, vegetables and even cranberries, in the best New England tradition, with no particular date, was celebrated according to local custom in the different colonies. And that is pretty much the way things were up until the Revolutionary War.

In December of 1777, General George Washington proclaimed a special "day of Thanksgiving" to celebrate the victory of the Americans over the British at the Battle of Saratoga.

Twelve years later, the newly elected President George Washington declared a proclamation naming Thursday, November 26th as the first *Official National Day of Thanksgiving.* John Adams followed suit with a similar proclamation. Thomas Jefferson did not. James Madison renewed the tradition, but for the most part, Thanksgiving was left up to the individual States until the time of the Civil War.

Then, in October of 1863, President Abraham Lincoln declared that the last Thursday of November should be set aside for Thanksgiving in part to *"fervently implore the interposition of the Almighty Hand to heal the wounds of the nation."* And that became the new tradition until the year 1939, when something changed.

In 1939, Franklin Roosevelt was president and the United States was in the middle of the Great Depression. It also happened that, in 1939, November had five Thursdays. It usually has four. But that year, if tradition held, Thanksgiving would not take place until the very end of the month. At that time, just as today, Thanksgiving was generally seen as the start of the Christmas shopping season. (It still marks the official kickoff, but that date seems to keep moving its way back toward the end of Halloween)

Anyway, President Roosevelt wanted to move Thanksgiving back a week to help stimulate the economy in hard times, but soon discovered that tradition is a hard thing to fight. The Republicans hated the idea of moving the date back a week and said so loudly. It got to be so political that November 30th of that year was called the Republican Thanksgiving and the earlier November 23rd was called the Democrat Thanksgiving, or what some called *FranksGiving* either in honor of or condemnation of President Roosevelt. (And we think politics is fierce today.) Some of the hesitation over which date to use was also caused by college football schedules, which traditionally held that teams played their final games on the day after Thanksgiving.

A lot of people went along with the earlier date. Merchants were only too happy to comply. And, in fact, the idea went over well enough that the next year, FDR moved Thanksgiving up <u>another week</u> to the third Thursday in November. For the record, twenty-three states went along with the President, twenty-two did not and three states celebrated both.

Finally, Congress got into the act, probably fearing that if Roosevelt lived long enough he'd move Thanksgiving back to the middle of the summer, and in December of 1941, the <u>official</u> Thanksgiving holiday was established as the 4th Thursday in November. And that's the way it has been...officially...ever since.

Happy Thanksgiving everybody.

Ho Ho Ho

As we approach Christmas, I thought it would be fun to explore one of the endearing traditions of the season; that of the jolly old man in the red suit who is the symbol of much of the joy of giving that is Christmas.

Of course, Christmas, in the religious sense, is not really about toys and parties. It is, first and foremost, the Christian celebration of the birth of Jesus. But what about the non-biblical figure that we include around Christmas. The figure that goes by various names, Kriss Kringle, St. Nicholas and, Santa Claus? Where do they all come from?

One of the most curious facts about Santa Claus is found in the name, Kriss Kringle, which is actually an alteration of the German word, Kristkind or *Christ child*. It's an ironic change because Kristkind was proposed by the protestant reformer, Martin Luther, who believed that the centuries-old tradition of Santa Claus had strayed entirely too far from the original meaning of Christmas; namely the birth of Jesus. Over time, the word Kristkind....morphed into KristKindl and eventually evolved into the gift-giver called Kriss Kringle, a figure who has become synonymous with the very Santa Claus that Martin Luther had objected to in the first place.

But the real story of Santa Claus takes us to the ancient world of what is now Turkey and the former Greek village of, Patara. In the late 3rd century, a young man by the name of, Nicholas, was born to wealthy parents who were devout Christians and raised their son in the same tradition. But, when he was a young man, Nicholas lost his parents in an epidemic. The only consolation was that he had received a sizable inheritance from his father and would probably have been able to live out his life in relative comfort.

But, instead, Nicholas followed the teachings of his faith and decided to, in the words of Jesus, "sell your possessions and give to the poor." (Luke 12:33). And give, he did. He used his entire inheritance to help the poor, the sick and those who had suffered in some way. He devoted his life to the Christian faith and was eventually made the Bishop of nearby Myra. In the Catholic tradition, Nicholas is considered the patron saint of sailors, and the protector of children.

There are many stories as to the generosity of Nicholas of Myra, one of which is directly tied to a Christmas tradition that we sill observe today.

In ancient times, when a young woman was to be married, it was expected that her father would provide the bridegroom with a dowry; a financial offering of some sort that would encourage a young man to take a wife. It's actually the reason that, in modern times, the father of the bride is still expected to pay for the lion's share of a wedding.

The story is told of three young women whose father could not afford a dowry for them, which meant that, in all probability, they would never marry, and would likely be sold as slaves. But they were not sold into slavery. Instead, on three separate occasions, bags of gold mysteriously ended up in the home of the three; enough to provide a generous dowry for each of them. What's more, the bags of gold, presumably thrown through the window, landed in stockings that had been hung over the fireplace to dry. And that is where we get the tradition of hanging Christmas stockings for treats and goodies. (I think I would prefer the gold)

It is this theme of gift-giving and generosity that has been handed down from one generation to the next over the last many centuries, in various forms in different nations across the entire realm of Christendom.

One of those traditions comes to us from the Netherlands, where the name and the figure of St. Nicholas of Myra would eventually evolve and transform itself into the character that the Dutch referred to as, *Sinterklaas,* which as you can easily hear, is the basis for our Santa Claus.

But the story doesn't end there.

Historical paintings of the image of St. Nicholas reflect his position as Bishop of Myra and they look like, well, a bishop; nothing like what we think of as Santa Claus

Now, fast forward to the year 1808 and Washington Irving's satirical, *History of New York,* where the image of Sinterklaas had been modernized to something close to the modern-day image of a friendly Dutchman carrying toys and treats on a sled pulled by eight reindeer. Irving's story was followed by the publication in 1822 of Clement Moore's poem, *A visit from St. Nicholas* or what we know as, *The Night Before Christmas;* a story which reinforced the image of Santa.

But the image changed again in 1863, in the middle of the American Civil War, when the January edition of Harper's Weekly magazine appeared with a now famous, smaller, somewhat elf-like cartoon figure of St. Nick that was the creation an artist by the name of Thomas Nast. Nast is also remembered as the creator of the civil war image of "Uncle Sam."

The original Nast, "Santa" appeared with a beard as he does today, but dressed in a suit that was fashioned from the flag of the United States; a shirt festooned with the stars of Old Glory, worn atop a pair of striped trousers. Nast was a supporter of the Union and apparently, so was Santa Claus. Nast would eventually dress Santa in a red suit that is more in line with our modern image.

But that's still not exactly the Santa that we see everywhere. That jolly old fat man in a red suit and hat with the traditional white fur trim around the edges comes to us from, of all places, the Coca Cola Company, who commissioned an artist by the name of Haddon Sundblum to show the jolly gift-giver having an ice cold Coca Cola in the middle of the winter. Coca Cola wanted to re-position itself as something that could be enjoyed throughout the year, not just in the summertime. And so, in the 1920's, Santa, now dressed in the familiar red and white that we expect whenever we go into a department store, started appearing in full page magazine ads enjoying a quick bottle of Coke on his way to deliver toys from the North Pole. Sundblum and his contemporary, Norman Rockwell, both borrowed heavily from the Nast image, and somewhere from the three of them is the image of St. Nicholas that most of us recognize today.

And that's the story of a young boy named Nicholas, who became known as the protector of children, whose Christian faith and generosity ended in sainthood, and in whose honor most Christians continue the tradition of anonymous gifts left by an ever-smiling grandfatherly figure called Kriss Kringle or St. Nick or Sinterklaas or Santa Claus riding on a sleigh, pulled by **nine** reindeer... if you count Rudolf.

Merry Christmas everybody!

An Homage to Golf

Every year, as the spring arrives and we emerge from the cold and frostbitten days of winter, we take both delight and comfort as the first buds of renewal appear, innocent and tenuous, on the branches of the long slumbering trees. Now, as we pass out of March, when as Dickens wrote, "the sun shines hot and the wind blows cold: when it is summer in the light, and winter in the shade", we finally find ourselves in April, having met the test of winter; a test to see if we are worthy of the bounty and the promise of the rest of the year

If you are a fan of the game of golf, then today's story may have a certain magical appeal. Then again, if golf is just a silly game played by retired people or as Mark Twain called it, "a good walk spoiled", then this story will likely fall on deaf ears. For those who love it, golf has an appeal and a mystery all of its own, a game that, in the words of the fictional Bagger Vance, "can't be won, only played."

And, commencing every first week in April, a uniquely American tradition repeats itself in a ritual that has been replayed in all but three years since 1934.

It was in April of 1934 that something happened for the first time ever. An elite group of professional and amateur sportsmen made its way to the warm climes of Augusta, in the state of Georgia just shy of the South Carolina border. They had come to the site of what was once an indigo plantation; a plot of land that had only recently been transformed into a landscaping wonder, The Augusta National Golf Club.

The group had come by invitation...to play in a tournament known at the time as the Augusta National Invitational. Five years later, in 1939, it would be given the name by which we all know it today and would become the annual venue of one of the most coveted prizes in the world of golf. Among the so called "Majors" of professional golf, it is the only one that is always played on the same course; a course, meticulously designed by the great golf architect, Alister McKenzie, with the help of the legendary Bobby Jones and financier Clifford Roberts.

It had been Bobby Jones's dream to build a golf course after his retirement from the game. Jones, the seemingly flawless amateur, who played with the greatest golfers of the 1920's as something of a part-time occupation while practicing law, wanted to create something special, something that would be a monument to the game that he so dearly loved. In that, he would succeed as no other before him. Because what came from his vision is a golf course that is consistently ranked as the greatest in all the world.

And, along with the course, comes the tournament that stands apart from all others. It is unique for its geographical and architectural landmarks; The Eisenhower tree, The Hogan Bridge that crosses Rae's Creek, Magnolia Lane, The Crow's Nest where the top amateur players are invited to stay during the tournament. And, of course, Amen Corner, a part of the course that has been the scene of much of golf's heartbreak and jubilation over many years.

Of course, one of the tournament's lasting traditions is in the wearing of a green jacket, a single-breasted blazer that is now presented to the winner of the competition each year. That was not always the case. Green jackets were originally purchased from the Brooks Uniform Company in New York City, not as a prize to the victor, but rather as a means of identifying the members of the club, who were on hand to answer questions from the many fans attending the tournament.

Speaking of fans, broadcasters rarely refer to them as such. In accordance with strict rules set up by the Club, fans or spectators are referred to as *patrons*. The rough is always referred to as, *the second cut*, another house rule. The rules are self-imposed by CBS which has broadcast the event since 1956. The CBS contract is renewed annually which assures that tournament directors will call the shots. The rules are so strict that some sports announcers have been banned from the tournament; notably, Emmy-award winner, Jack Whitaker, in 1966 for calling the fans a mob, and Gary McCord in 1994 for saying that the 17th green was, "so fast it appeared to be bikini-waxed."

The first entry on the list of tournament winners went to Horton Smith in 1934. He edged out Craig Woods by two strokes and went home with prize money totaling fifteen <u>hundred</u> dollars. He would go on to win a second time a couple of years later. From that point on, the list of winners is populated by all of the notables in the game; Sam Snead, Ben Hogan, Arnold Palmer, Jack Nicklaus, Tom Watson, Tiger Woods and at this writing by Phil Michelson, who won in 2010[1]. Phil's paycheck was a little larger than Horton Smith's, coming in at One million, three hundred fifty thousand dollars. That's not counting the cost of the green jacket.

For the record, it was Sam Snead who donned the Green Jacket for the first time in 1949 in recognition of his victory, and that has been the tradition ever since.

Jack Nicklaus holds the title for most tournament victories at six, a feat that was once thought to be in danger of being matched by Tiger Woods, but now seems more and more impressive as Tiger's game has faltered and the passage of time makes the accomplishment seem all that more elusive.

But, regardless of who wins this year or or in the years to come, this singular event, with its rich history, its traditions, its dogwoods, junipers and azaleas, its culture and its controversies, marks the annual renewal of a quest that for most of us is but a dream.

It is a tournament eloquently described in just two words:

The Masters.

(first recorded in April of 2011)

1) The 2011 winner was South African Charl Schwartzel

Thirteen Days

Today's story is not about a business or an individual. It is about an historical event; an event that took place over the span of thirteen days in October of 1962 that brought the world to the brink of disaster.

Our story actually begins in the pre-dawn hours of the morning of July 16, 1945, when the skies over the White Sands of the State of New Mexico were illuminated, as one observer remarked, brighter than daylight, as military and scientific personnel witnessed the first ever atomic explosion. It was the one and only test firing of a weapon that three weeks later would be used not once, but twice on the Empire of Japan, thus bringing an end to the Second World War.

For a time, the United States held sole possession of atomic weapons. It was to be a short-lived monopoly. The blueprints for this most guarded of military secrets had been handed over to the Soviet Union by a ring of spies, some of whom truly believed that a one-sided ownership of nuclear weapons was more dangerous than an evenly-weighted balance of power. Regardless of motivation, on August 29th, 1949, the Soviet Union detonated its first nuclear weapon and the world found itself at the beginning of an arms race that would last for another forty years.

The destructive power of the earliest of atomic weapons had been enough to completely level the Japanese cities of Hiroshima and

Nagasaki, but those weapons were mere firecrackers compared to what was to come in fairly short order. The Hydrogen bomb was soon perfected by both sides, and by the early 1950's, two great nations were working feverishly to keep up with one another.

The nuclear arms race was based, at first, on a traditional concept of balance of power, a simple idea that as long as both sides are relatively equal in their weapons systems a stalemate will follow that will, ironically, prevent war. This was further refined into a concept known as, *"MAD,"* an acronym for *mutual assured destruction*; a term coined by Hungarian-born mathematician, John Von Neumann, and based on the idea that a nuclear attack on America would be met without hesitation by a counterattack on the Soviet Union, thus assuring the annihilation of both sides. As implausible as it might sound, it has kept the world from blowing itself up for more than half a century.

But making *MAD* work depends on knowing how many bombs the other side has, and in the 1950's neither side was about to send an inventory list to the other, although, in hindsight, it might have been a good idea.

Instead, the intelligence agencies of the East and the West engaged in a never-ending vigil to keep up with the bomb count.

One of the measures employed by the U.S. was the use of a radical spy plane that made its debut in 1955. Called the U-2, it was built by the Lockheed Corporation and was able to fly at altitudes of roughly 70,000 feet; a height believed to be out of reach of the Russian defense system. The optical cameras on the U-2 were state-of-the art, able to distinguish objects less than a yard wide from nearly fourteen miles above the earth. The planes routinely flew over Russian airspace until one piloted by Francis Gary Powers was knocked out of the sky. That put and end to the flights over Russia, but there was still a plot of land ninety miles southeast of Florida that kept the U-2's busy; the island nation of Cuba.

On October 14, 1962, a U-2 flight over Cuba revealed something that sent a shock wave through the halls of the American government; the Soviet Union was installing medium-range intercontinental ballistic missiles on the island. If they became operational, fully two thirds of the U.S. mainland would be within their reach with virtually no advance warning. The balance of power was in jeopardy.

Letting the missiles stay in Cuba would place a nuclear *sword of Damocles* over the head of every future American government. Removing them would risk global nuclear war.

After eight days of back and forth conferences between the White House and the Pentagon, debating whether or not to invade Cuba and risk almost certain retaliation from the Soviet Union, President John F. Kennedy decided to enforce what he called a *"quarantine"* of weapons delivered to Cuba. It was effectively a naval blockade, but the <u>word "blockade"</u> is considered an act of war under international law, so the action was called a quarantine.

On the evening of October 22nd 1962, President Kennedy addressed the nation with words that still seem chilling today:

Good evening, my fellow citizens:

This Government, as promised, has maintained the closest surveillance of the Soviet military buildup on the island of Cuba. Within the past week, unmistakable evidence has established the fact that a series of offensive missile sites is now in preparation on that imprisoned island. The purpose of these bases can be none other than to provide a nuclear strike capability against the Western Hemisphere...

...To halt this offensive buildup a strict quarantine on all offensive military equipment under shipment to Cuba is being initiated. All ships of any kind bound for Cuba from whatever nation or port will, if found to contain cargoes of offensive weapons, be turned back. This quarantine will be extended, if needed, to other types of cargo and carriers. We are not at this time, however, denying the necessities of life as the Soviets attempted to do in their Berlin blockade of 1948...

...It shall be the policy of this nation to regard any nuclear missile launched from Cuba against any nation in the Western Hemisphere as an attack by the Soviet Union on the United States, requiring a full retaliatory response upon the Soviet Union...

Even after the President's speech, as the world held its breath, a group of Soviet cargo ships continued to sail toward an imaginary line in the Atlantic Ocean with no signs of hesitation. On and on into the night and the early morning they continued to move toward the line. The threat of military confrontation on the high seas was a reality of which neither side knew the outcome. Two great superpowers were staring each other in the face, and then finally, the Soviets blinked. The Russian freighters, slowed, changed course and turned around. It was the ultimate test of brinkmanship; the closest the world has ever come to nuclear war and, fortunately, has never been repeated.

Within days, by public and private agreements, the Russian missiles and warheads were dismantled and removed, but the scare would prompt American citizens to build home bomb shelters by the tens of thousands.

It happened forty-nine years ago this week; an incident known forever as the thirteen days of...

The Cuban Missile Crisis.

(first broadcast on October 22, 2011)

The Unlocked Door

(originally recorded August 10, 2011)

Yesterday, August 9th marked the 47th anniversary of something that had never before happened in history; a sitting President of the United States would resign the office of the Presidency. It would alter the course of American politics and create a power shift, the impact of which can still be felt today.

If you've never been to our nation's capitol, it's worth the trip. It is best enjoyed in the spring before it gets too hot. By July, it is close to unbearable, so unbearable that for most of our nation's history, the job of being a member of Congress was basically a part time job. That changed in the 1930's when the Roosevelt administration put air-conditioning into the halls of Congress as part of a jobs program during the Great Depression. And, for better or for worse, since that time, Senators and Representatives have been able to make their mischief pretty much all year long.

But, in the springtime, Washington is beautiful; The White House, The Washington, Lincoln and Jefferson Memorials, Arlington National Cemetery, the cherry blossoms in full bloom, and the inspired layout of the city as envisioned in the late 1700's by architect, Pierre L'Enfant.

Within the city, in a place called *Foggy Bottom* stands an apartment and office complex that overlooks the Potomac River; a group of buildings whose name has become part of the American language and has become a suffix that stands for political scandal the world over.

On the night of June 17, 1972, five men (Virgilio González, Bernard Barker, James W. McCord, Jr., Eugenio Martínez, and Frank Sturgis) were caught red-handed in the act of committing a burglary. But it wasn't an ordinary burglary and these weren't your ordinary burglars. They weren't looking for money. Instead, they were on a reconnaissance mission; a mission to discover what secrets they could find about possible candidates seeking the Democratic Party's nomination for the Office of President in the upcoming November election.

The men were discovered during a routine check of the premises by a security guard named, Frank Wills. Wills had noticed that someone had taped the latch of an outside door to prevent it locking as it closed.

At first, Wills thought little of the tape, thinking it had been placed by movers to eliminate the hassle of unlocking the door. So he removed the tape. Sometime later, he discovered that the tape had magically re-appeared, and that's when he made a phone call.

The Washington D.C. Police were summoned, and five men spent the night in jail. A subsequent investigation by the FBI would discover that two of the burglars were connected to the Nixon Administration, almost directly to the White House itself. The burglars had been paid from a slush fund run by two White House operatives, E. Howard Hunt and G. Gordon Liddy.

The tangled web of intrigue and deceit would lead two investigative reporters, Bob Woodward and Carl Bernstein of the Washington Post, on a journalistic odyssey that would eventually lead to Senate Hearings held in full view of worldwide television audiences during the summer of 1973.

The complete list of the characters of the conspiracy is too large to enumerate in this simple story, but a few of the notables were former

Attorney General of the United States, John Mitchell, The President's head of staff Bob Haldeman, and special advisers John Erlichman and John Dean. Dean would be the first to come clean and admit to the conspiracy.

As the weeks and months dragged on, in the middle of what at the time seemed like a lot of smoke with no smoking gun, the President of the United States appeared on prime-time television to clear his good name, and looking straight into the camera, declared that, "people have got to know whether or not their president's a crook, well I'm not a crook."

It was a baldfaced lie, a tragic attempt to overwhelm an often forgiving public. It would be the statement for which Richard Nixon, a man who had accomplished so much in his turbulent political career, would never be forgiven.

The last straw would come in two phases.

When John Erlichman and Bob Haldeman left the White House under indictment, President Nixon asked for the resignation of Attorney General Richard Kleindienst. That same day, Nixon appointed Elliot Richardson as the new AG. Feeling the heat from political leaders and the Washington Post, Nixon authorized Elliot Richardson to appoint a special prosecutor named, Archibald Cox, to "investigate" the whole mess that by now bore the name of the apartment and complex where it all started.

Nixon undoubtedly hoped that Archibald Cox either couldn't get to the bottom of things or wouldn't. He was wrong.

It all started to unravel when a minor White House aide, Alexander Butterfield, casually mentioned a recording system that tape-recorded all conversations in the oval office. Special prosecutor Cox asked for the tapes of Nixon's conversations and Nixon refused. Instead, the

President ordered Attorney General Richardson to fire Cox, who had clearly become a pain in the rear. Rather than carry out the order, Richardson resigned. So, President Nixon ordered then Solicitor General, Robert Bourke, to fire Cox, which he did, and in doing so destroyed any chance of ever sitting on the Supreme Court, to which he would be later nominated.

The Supreme Court finally ordered the President to hand over the tapes to Congress, only to discover that apart from some rather colorful language, something was missing. There was an eighteen and a half minute gap on one of the tapes. What might have been the smoking gun had been <u>mysteriously</u> erased.

Finally, enough was enough. The burglary, the cover-up, the tail of lies, the late night firings and finally the erased audio tape were too much for an increasingly angered public and Congress to take.

On the evening of August 8, 1974, facing almost certain Impeachment by the House of Representatives, a beleaguered and defeated Richard Milhous Nixon said something never before spoken to the American people;

" I shall resign the presidency effective at noon tomorrow."

It was the end of an ordeal that those who were witnesses to history will never forget. An ordeal that had begun just two years earlier when a security guard noticed a piece of tape on a door, at an office complex known as....

The Watergate.

One Day in September

(originally broadcast on 9/9/2011)

As we approach the tenth anniversary of the attacks on the World Trade Center and Washington D.C., I thought it would be appropriate to tell today's story, which, as it turns out, has an origin whose date is eerily coincidental.

Perhaps no date will be remembered as definitively as September 11th, 2001, a date that for most Americans now living will forever eclipse the "date that will live in infamy" of December 7th, 1941... so declared by Franklin Roosevelt some seventy years earlier. The images of the smoldering and then falling twin towers of New York's World Trade Center are forever etched in the memories of all who saw them on that fateful day.

This is the story of an island. Of all the islands in the world, only a handful stand out; Great Britain, Ireland and Japan. Australia, if you're counting continents. Of course, there's Greenland and Iceland, the Hawaiian Islands and the twins that make up New Zealand, but after that, the rest all seem to blur.

I intentionally left out the one island that is probably the most storied in the world. It has been written into song and into fable. It has been the home of the original "subway series" between baseball teams known as the Giants and the Yankees (and the Mets). The home of the Polo Grounds and Wall Street and Broadway, Times Square, Tiffany's and Central Park. It is what we think of when we talk or write about New York City. Not Queens, or Brooklyn or the Bronx. It is the island that songwriter Stephen Sondheim spoke of when he wrote, "smoke on your pipe and put that in." The island that rhymes with Staten Island, too.

The Island to which Brooklyn was connected by the Great Bridge in 1876; the island after whose lower end the Bowery Boys were named.

It is where you, "take the A-Train to get to Sugar Hill in Harlem" and the home of Hell's Kitchen and the Five Points and other areas that Humphrey Bogart advised the German Major Strassner to avoid in the film, *Casablanca*. A sliver of land that stretches some thirteen miles from north to south and is barely two miles wide as it sits between the Hudson and East rivers.

From the European point of view, it was discovered by the Dutch navigator, Henry Hudson. Of course, the native American peoples who inhabited the land long before the arrival of the white man were only too familiar with its subtle hills and beautiful vistas.

Hudson had originally been commissioned by the English, Muscovy Company, to find the elusive Northwest Passage; a northerly shortcut to the riches of the Far East. Hudson would never accomplish the impossible goal.

He would die trying; an ignominious death along with his son and eight shipmates who would be cast adrift in a small boat in the vast inland sea that is now called Hudson Bay; the victims of a mutinous crew who, in the year 1611, wanted no more of Hudson and his quest for fame and fortune. It was a sad and ghostly end to a career that had often been marked by hardship and frustration.

But, two years earlier, in better and happier times, Hudson had captained the legendary sailing ship, *Half Moon*, finding his way to the mouth of the river that now bears his name and dropping anchor on the very date that would become indelibly imprinted on the collective memory of every American, nearly four hundred years later.

Because, it was on one late summer's day in the first weeks of September, on a voyage full of hope and promise, that this Dutch explorer would disembark from the *Half Moon* and become the first European to set foot on the island that would become home to the colony of New Amsterdam, and later to the steel and concrete architectural wonder that we call New York City.

This day, September 11th, would mark a beginning for western explorers, and sadly, the beginning of the end for the people who had been there all along; the native inhabitants known as the Algonquins, who had originally given the name to this place. This place upon whose hard and rocky shore the writer H.L. Mencken wrote that, "every great wave of populism that rises up from the prairie is dashed to spray".

For on that day, as the rich warm breeze of the summer wind drifted over the vacant island that would one day be home to the Twin Towers of the World Trade Center, before there was the Empire State Building or Radio City, or Madison Square Garden; before there was the Statue of Liberty or Carnegie Hall, or the Great Bridge or any of the myriad monuments to the aspirations and ingenuity of mankind; before there was any of it, as the sun set on the eleventh day of September, in the year 1609, the only traces that could be found of western civilization would be the footprints of strangers, left in the sand on the shore of the place whose name means, "the island of many hills." The island the natives called,

Manhattan.

About the author

R. Haywood (Woody) Vincent, Jr. is an entrepreneur, radio talk show host and former advertising agency executive, with an extensive knowledge of business, the stock market and all things trivial.

He graduated from Newton North High School in Newtonville, Massachusetts, and later attended the University of Colorado where he received his Bachelor of Arts Degree in Anthropology.

He is currently the co-host of the *Business for Breakfast* radio program which broadcasts daily in the Denver area and on several other radio stations throughout the state of Colorado.

He is the father of three grown children, an avid golfer and spends much of his time looking after a Boston Terrier named Marty, whom he adopted from a rescue organization in 2009.

This is his first book.

Acknowledgments

Every effort has been made to cite correct trademark ownership in the creation of this book. Wherever possible I have used the current trademark information as listed at the U.S. Patent and Trademark Office whose website proved to be an invaluable tool in doing the research for *What's In A Name*.

Trademark acknowledgments:

Amen Corner® is a registered trademark of Augusta National, Inc.
Ameritrade® is a registered trademark of Ameritrade IP Company, Inc.
Amana® is a registered trademark of Maytag Properties, LLC
Aunt Jemima® is a registered trademark of The Quaker Oats Company
Band-Aid® is a registered trademark of Johnson and Johnson
Aveeno®, Benadryl®,Bengay®, Cortaid®, Listerine®, Mylanta®,
Neutrogena®, Rogaine®, Sudafed® and Tylenol®, and are all registered trademarks of Johnson and Johnson
Baldwin® is a registered trademark of Baldwin Piano, Inc.
Balkan Sobranie is a registered trademark of Gallaher Limited
Barbie® is a registered trademark of Mattel, Inc.
Betty Crocker® is a registered trademark of General Mills, Inc
Blaupunkt® is a registered trademark of ED Enterprises AG
Bosendorfer® is a registered trademark of P.S.K Beteiligungsverwaltung GMBH
Charlie Tuna® is a registered trademark of Star-Kist Foods, Inc.
Chickering® is a registered trademark of The Wurlitzer Company
Coke® is a registered trademark of The Coca-Cola Company
Coca-Cola® is a registered trademark of The Coca-Cola Company
Chiclets® is a registered trademark of Kraft Foods Global Brands LLC
Dom Perignon® is a registered trademark of Moet Hennessy USA, Inc.
DuPont® is a registered trademark of E.I. Du Pont de Nemours and Company
Nylon®, Teflon®, Kevlar®, Mylar®, Lycra® and Corian® are all registered trademarks of E.I. Du Pont de Nemours and Company
Edsel® is a registered trademark of the Ford Motor Company
Fedex® is a registered trademark of Federal Express Corporation

Frigidaire® is a registered trademark of Electrolux Home Products, Inc.

Frisbee® is a registered trademark of Wham-O, Inc.

Gillette® is a registered trademark of The Gillette Company

Google® is a registered trademark of Google, Inc.

Gore-Tex® is a registered trademark of W.L. Gore and Associates

Grape Nuts® is a registered trademark of Kraft Foods Holdings, Inc.

The Guinness Book of World Records® is a registered trademark of Guinness World Records Limited

Harley-Davidson® is a registered trademark of H-D Michigan, LLC

Home Shopping Network® is a registered trademark of Home Shopping Network, Inc.

IBM® is a registered trademark of International Business Machines, Inc.

Jack Daniels® is a registered trademark of Jack Daniel's Properties, Inc.

Jaguar® is a registered trademark of Jaguar Cars Limited

John Deere® is a registered trademark of Deere and Company

Kodak® is a registered trademark of Eastman Kodak Company

Kmart® is a registered trademark of Sears Brands, LLC

The Masters® is a registered trademark of Augusta National, Inc.

Mercedes-Benz® is a registered trademark of Daimler, A.G.

Monopoly® is a registered trademark of Hasbro, Inc.

Monsanto® is a registered trademark of Monsanto Technology LLC

Netflix® is a registered trademark of Netflix, Inc.

Nutrasweet® is a registered trademark of Nutra Sweet Property Holding, Inc.

Pep Boys® is a registered trademark of The Pep Boys Manny, Moe & Jack of California

Pine Sol® is a registered trademark of The Clorox Company

Polo® is a registered trademark of PRL USA Holdings, Inc.

Polo Ralph Lauren® is a registered trademark of PRL USA Holdings, Inc.

Rolex® is a registered trademark of Rolex Watch USA, Inc.

Roundup® is a registered trademark of Monsanto Technology LLC

Scrabble® is a registered trademark of Hasbro, Inc.

Splenda® is a registered trademark of McNeil Nutritionals, LLC

Stainmaster® is a registered trademark of E.I du Pont de Nemours and Company

Steinway® is a registered trademark of Steinway and Sons

The Instrument of the Immortals® is a registered trademark of Steinway and Sons

Starbucks® is a registered trademark of Starbucks Corporation

Tabasco® is a registered trademark of McIllhenny Company

Teflon® is a registered trademark of E.I. Du Pont de Nemours and Company

The Waldorf-Astoria® is a registered trademark of HLT Domestic IP LLC

Uncle Ben's® is a registered trademark of Uncle Ben's, Incorporated

Weed-B-Gon® is a registered trademark of The Scotts Company LLC

Wendy's® is a registered trademark of Oldemark LLC
Westinghouse® is a registered trademark of Westinghouse Air Brake
    Technologies
Winchester® is a registered trademark of Olin Corporation
Juicy Fruit®, Spearmint®, Doublemint® and Big Red® are registered
trademarks of Wm. Wrigley Jr. Company
Yamaha® is a registered trademark of Yamaha Corporation

Source Material:

This book is meant to be a journalistic attempt at entertainment, and is not offered as a work of academic scholarship. As I mentioned in my introductory remarks, I have relied on company websites for the bulk of the material in this book. Most large companies have taken the time to create extensive time lines for anyone who wishes to learn about them. In other cases, I have made extensive use of the online encyclopedia, Wikipedia, with the understanding that, as Wikipedia itself states,

"As with any source, especially one of unknown authorship, you should be wary and independently verify the accuracy of Wikipedia information if possible. For many purposes, but particularly in academia, Wikipedia may not be an acceptable source; indeed, some professors and teachers may reject Wikipedia-sourced material completely."

With that said, if you wish to find further information on any or all the stories, Wikipedia. and Encyclopedia Britannica Online are valuable sources of information, and within their articles you will find ample footnotes and references. The material contained herein, therefore, is believed to be reliable and accurate, but no guarantee is made as to its absolute accuracy.--wv